The Taste of Shabbos

The Taste

A PROJECT OF AISH HATORAH WOMEN'S ORGANIZATION

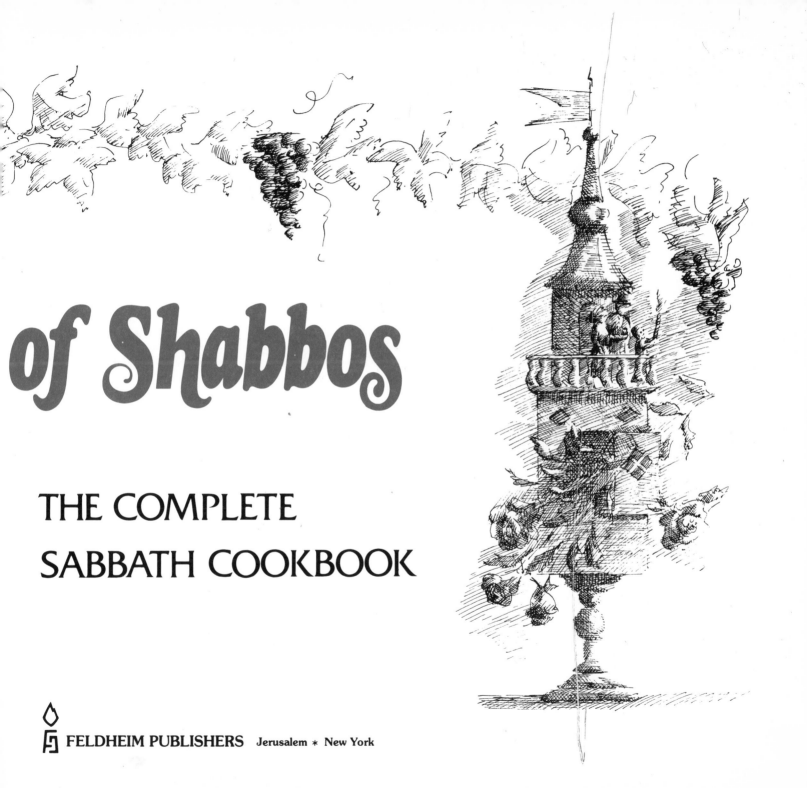

# of Shabbos

THE COMPLETE
SABBATH COOKBOOK

FELDHEIM PUBLISHERS   Jerusalem * New York

*This book contains words of Torah and
should be treated with proper respect.*

Aish HaTorah
College of Jewish Studies

A PROJECT OF AISH HATORAH
WOMEN'S ORGANIZATION

ISBN 0-87306-426-7
Copyright © 1987 by
Aish HaTorah Women's Organization
P.O.B. 14149
Jewish Quarter, Old City
Jerusalem, Israel

Second, corrected edition, 1988

Cover: Yael Hershberg
Illustrations: Yael Hershberg, Malka Schallheim
Graphics and Layout: Malka Schallheim
Typesetting: Astronel, Jerusalem
Inside Aish HaTorah Layout: Diane Liff
Photographs: Moshe Hoffman

Published by
Philipp Feldheim, Inc.
200 Airport Executive Park
Spring Valley, NY 10977

Feldheim Publishers, Ltd.
POB 6525 / Jerusalem, Israel

Printed in Israel

Table of Contents

This book is dedicated to
those Jewish women throughout history –
past, present and future –
who have through their wisdom and devotion
preserved the Jewish home and community
and ushered in weekly
the taste and light of Shabbos.

Preface

It is with great pleasure that we present this cookbook in the hope that it will help make the taste of Shabbos richer for you, your family and guests.

Before using our cookbook, please be advised that references to matters of Jewish law (*halachah*) sometimes appear. However, detailed explanations of the laws of the Sabbath or of *kashruth*, methods for inspecting fruits and vegetables for insects, and all other *halachoth* are beyond the scope of this book. All these are subjects which the homemaker must study carefully and review regularly.

We recommend the following books for home study:

1. *The Sabbath*, Grunfeld, Fourth Edition, Feldheim, Jerusalem, 1981.
2. *Shemirath Shabbath*, Neuwirth, Feldheim, Jerusalem, 1984.
3. *Practical Guide to Kashruth*, Wagschal, Feldheim, Jerusalem, 1984.
4. *The NEW Care of Children on Shabbos and Yom Tov*, Wagschal, Feldheim, Jerusalem, 1985.
5. *The Jew and His Home*, Kitov, Shengold, New York, 1985.

All our recipes for Sabbath food should be prepared completely before the Sabbath begins. There are three main Sabbath meals: Friday night, Sabbath morning and Sabbath afternoon. After Sabbath, a fourth meal — *Melaveh Malkah* — is served. (*Melaveh Malkah* preparations may be made after the Sabbath ends.) To keep foods warm for the Friday night meal, and to keep cholent or appropriate kugels hot until the morning meal, a hotplate or covered flame must be set up before candlelighting. The flame may be covered with an asbestos pad or a sheet of metal (*blech*) and the hot food placed on it.

Many fruits, vegetables and grains must be inspected to be sure that they are not infested with insects. The foods in question as well as the techniques for checking vary among the different countries and seasons — thus one must keep up with the local situation.

The Land of Israel is holy and so is its produce. Before eating anything grown in *Eretz Yisrael*, the different *terumoth* and *maaseroth* mentioned in the Torah must be assigned and their requirements carried out. If one is not certain whether this has already been done, *halachah* calls for designating all *terumoth* and *maaseroth*, without the *brachah*. *Maaser sheni* — the tithe that was to be brought to Jerusalem — must be redeemed with a coin set aside for that purpose. This also applies outside of *Eretz Yisrael*, in the case of fruits or vegetables grown in *Eretz Yisrael*. The Jewish home should therefore possess the necessary text and coin to be used for foods without reliable certification indicating that tithes were already properly taken.

It is important to note that fruits and vegetables grown in *Eretz Yisrael* are sometimes affected by the laws of *shmittah*, rendering them unusable for certain recipes, or requiring that they undergo special handling. For further details, we recommend the *Guide for the Year of Sh'mittah*, Kahana, Feldheim, Jerusalem, 1986, and *Understanding Shmittoh*, Marchant, Feldheim, 1986.

In converting weights from pounds to kilograms and vice versa, we have approximated in accordance with packaging conventions. Suggested pan sizes are those used in the United States. "Cups" are 8 oz. American standard. Number of servings is approximate and will vary with circumstances.

A few words about transliteration: no other problem occupied the editors of this volume as much. Should the word be written Shabbos, Shabbat, or the Sabbath? And so on with all other words and expressions transliterated from our holy tongue. Dispersed to the far ends of the earth, Jews have developed different speech conventions (among other superficial differences) beneath which we remain, of course, a single people. Could we be faithful to that unity, be consistent, and maintain a degree of warmth in our transcription of these few words? In the end, we sacrificed consistency, choosing the spelling which seemed most right (or least wrong) *to us* in each context. We ask that each reader pronounce the words as she prefers, regardless of English spelling.

Recipes were collected from Jewish homemakers all over the world. We are grateful to all who contributed recipes, whether or not they were included in this final version.

Contributors include: Beth Ackerman, Emuna Braverman, Irma Charles, Aliza Cohen, Miriam Einseidler, ע״ה, Nechama Eisenblatt, Rivka Epstein, Robin Goldberg, Arleen Habshush, Alison Karpel, Shari Kaufman, Aliza Kramer, Malka Levine, Sheryl Meyer, Miryam Naki, Rena Novack, Sarah Orenbach, Devorah Plaut, Ruth Rosenberg, Leah Schechter, Mazal Schwartz, Sora Stein, Evelyn Sunray, Rivka Tal, Ilene Webb, Lottie Wilk, Shelly Willis

Special thanks to: Rochel Black, Sheira Cashman, Linda Dayan, Shoshana Dolgin, Miriam Eisler, Miriam Finkel, Sara Finkel, Ethel Krybus, Nehama Consuelo Nahmoud, Rebbetzin Denah Weinberg, and gourmet chef, Shalom Katz.

We thank Rabbi Akiva Yosef Eisenbach, author of *Ohr HaShabbos* and Rabbi Zelig Pliskin, author of *Love Your Neighbor*, for their kind permission to use and adapt material from their books.

We thank our publisher, Mr. Yaakov Feldheim, and Yaffa Ganz and Harvey Klineman for their advice and encouragement; and Rabbi Yitzchak Berkowitz for his invaluable halachic advice.

We hope you enjoy the *Taste of Shabbos* as much as we have enjoyed preparing it and sharing it with you.

Editorial Committee: Dvorah Eisenbach
Zelda Goldfield
Shifra Slater

The Taste of Shabbos

What is the taste of Shabbos? Elusive, special, unique — it is the secret ingredient in any dish prepared in honor of the Holy Sabbath. The nature of this seasoning, says Rabbi Yehoshua ben Chananiah, is that it will flavor only the food of one who keeps the Sabbath laws.

How can this be explained?

In the six days of Creation, the Creator brought into being all the material elements in our world. But material was not enough. The culmination came on the seventh day when all physical creative activity ceased, and the spiritual dimension was introduced. This was the Sabbath of Creation. Thus, the Sabbath concept is, theoretically, the property of the whole world, the heritage of all mankind.

And yet, we know that the Sabbath is a special gift, Divinely ordained for the Jewish people alone, so much so that our Sages tell us the Sabbath and Israel are like mates to one another.

Keeping the Sabbath, remembering it and sanctifying it — this is the unique triple obligation and opportunity afforded to the Jewish people. In fact, this multi-faceted *mitzvah* epitomizes the Jew's obligations, his very function on earth, and is considered the equivalent of all the other *mitzvoth*.

Let us try to understand why this is so.

The nations of the world adopted a pattern superficially similar to that of Creation: work six days a week, then have a day "off." The same prevailed where material and spiritual matters were concerned: after attending to food, shelter and clothing or career, culture and recreation, man took some time out to acknowledge his "religion." But this was a grievous misinterpretation of the significance of the Sabbath. Mankind had missed the point.

So a single nation, *Am Yisroel*, was selected to bear the responsibility for interpreting the patterns of creation. Taking us out of enslavement in Egypt, the Master of the Universe gave us His Torah, with instructions and guidelines to shape our every action and to give us insights into the basic truths behind creation itself. Sabbath then became a double reminder for the Jew. It reminds us not only of the work of Creation, but also of our exodus from Egypt — the point at which this Divine message was focused on the Jew alone.

This message is clarified for us through our commandments (*mitzvoth*). One after another, they illustrate the idea that the material world was created for spiritual purposes. Even the most concrete, the most physical, can and must be elevated to spiritual realms. Everything in the material world is a vehicle for serving the Creator — spiritual goal par excellence.

The Jew recognizes that all of Creation remained, in a sense, suspended until the seventh day. By introducing the spiritual dimension, the Creator imparted meaning to the material world. All at once, its components came to life retroactively. Thus, there can be no separation. The Sabbath is not a thing apart. "And G-d completed *with* the seventh day His work that He had made." The light of the Sabbath illuminates the entire week.

The proper blend of material and spiritual is the ultimate goal of man's existence. But he will lose sight of this truth if left to his own instruction. The Jew is more fortunate. The laws and regulations of Sabbath observance, in particular, epitomize this blending principle for him. The Sabbath — day of abstinence from concrete creative activity, day of spiritual refreshment, is honored and observed with the most tangible, physical preparations.

We call the Sabbath "delight" and define this very specifically: food and drink, special garments, fresh linens, and bodily rest. When these physical pleasures are the means to spiritual ends, all the seven days of Creation come into focus.

Only by striving to serve the Creator can we imbue an otherwise flat and tasteless world with transcendant life and genuine flavor. By preparing, each week, the most tempting and sumptuous food, not as an end in itself, but in service to the Master of the Universe, the Jew remembers his reason for being.

The special pleasure which the Jew derives from foods prepared for the Sabbath is therefore more than a merely gustatory sensation. It is the satisfaction which springs from aspiring to blend the elements of Creation in accordance with Divine will.

This is the taste of Shabbos.

"Whoever prepares before the Sabbath will eat on the Sabbath"

(Talmud Bavli)

Why Prepare? History and Halachah

Since the Children of Israel left Egypt nearly 3,500 years ago, their mothers have been busily preparing for the Sabbath Queen on Friday. In fact, Friday is designated as the special day on which we prepare for the Sabbath, as it is written, "See, G-d has given you the Sabbath, therefore He gives you on the sixth day bread for two days " (Exodus 16:29). By preparing their sustenance on the sixth day for the Sabbath, the Jews were enabled to rest completely on the Sabbath and devote the day to spiritual matters. "So the people rested on the seventh day " (Exodus 16:30).

Sabbath preparations may not have been too complicated in the desert encampments of the fledgling nation. All that was required was a short walk to collect a measure of manna, which not only tasted like honey cakes (or whatever one would want it to taste like, according to the Midrash), but was even hygienically packaged between two layers of freshly fallen dew!

Food preparation today is much more complicated for most women. The more we require, the more we perspire. Since cooking, baking, frying, shredding, chopping, mincing, kneading, and many other food-related activities are prohibited on the Sabbath, the Jewish homemaker plans and prepares all three Sabbath meals in advance, so that when the Sabbath Queen arrives, all preparations are completed. Then we, like our newly freed ancestors, are able to "rest on the seventh day."

Today's homemaker may well prefer to begin her preparations before Friday. Besides cooking and baking, there are planning, shopping, cleaning, studying, and even earning the money to pay the bills! All are bound up with arranging for our present day Sabbath double measure of manna. "Six days shall you work..." — all that we do during those six days is geared towards the culmination of the week, the Sabbath.

But Who Likes to Prepare?

How many months passed between the time of your engagement and your wedding? Did it seem like years — or did it fly past like just a few days? All the preparations! Learning, planning and shopping for the wedding and for your new abode; the hall, rabbi, guest list, menu, band, wedding gown, trousseau, apartment, furniture — how in the world did you get everything ready in time? It was a hectic period — but always full of excitement, glee and longing for that day when the ceremony would finally take place. In retrospect, we recall enjoying the weeks of preparation as well as the event itself.

The same is true of the Sabbath preparations. Although our efforts are aimed towards the culmination, we often find these efforts in themselves thoroughly pleasurable. Preparing menus, baking challah, arranging flowers, inviting guests, etc. can all be great fun. Even the less attractive chores can be made enjoyable if we keep in mind that we are doing them *lekovod Shabbos*, in honor of the Sabbath.

Our round-the-world, through-the-generations survey of preparation systems revealed that there are as many different approaches as there are homemakers.

Some tend towards a method like that of Shammai the Elder (a sage of the Mishnah), who began setting aside something for the Sabbath from the first day of the week. More recently, Rabbi Yosef Haim of Baghdad, author of *Ben Ish Hai* (5594-5669/1834-1909), reformulated this scheme by recommending that lists be made early in the week, and that cooking and cleaning be done by Thursday, so that Friday could be devoted to spiritual preparation for the Sabbath. The Ben Ish Hai emphasized that *mitzvoth* take place on two levels simultaneously — the spiritual and the physical. He offered three hints to facilitate our Sabbath preparations: make lists, rise early, and whatever you are doing, do it with *simchah* (joy).

At the other end of the spectrum, homemakers may be more like Hillel the Elder (contemporary and colleague of Shammai). She places her trust in G-d, confident that even if she leaves preparations for the end of the week, He will help her complete them. Some women leave all their preparations for Friday. This schedule may be suitable for a single person whose Sabbath preparations are not so involved, or for

the superwoman who lives next door. (May G-d grant her health and strength!)

Don't be surprised if you find yourself shifting or combining. Most homemakers fall somewhere in the middle of the two archetypes, varying their methods and systems at different times. Schedules change along with family situation, budget, time of year, and other factors.

And when twilight arrives on Friday, Jewish women everywhere breathlessly scurry to give those last minute touches, and kindling the Sabbath lights, welcome the Sabbath Queen.

Ten tried and true tips:

1. Make lists of what to buy and what to do, and cross things off as you do them.

2. Plan menus early in the week; don't overburden yourself with an elaborate menu plan. Simpler meals with a relaxed hostess are a better combination than fancy foods and an exhausted cook.

3. Leave nothing for Friday — there will be plenty to do anyway.

4. Play music or sing Sabbath songs while you work. Raising your *simchah* level will speed production.

5. Check your lists for opportunities to peel potatoes all at once for more than one recipe, slice all the onions in a single session, etc.

6. Check flour and legumes, etc. for insects the day before you will use them and refrigerate overnight. The next day you'll be ready to go!

7. Double your recipes for challah, cakes, kugels, gefilte fish. Use half this week and freeze the other half. This way you can increase the variety of foods on a subsequent Sabbath.

8. Give yourself a special reason to finish early — set a time by which you'll be ready to take an outing with the family, read the *parshah* (weekly Torah portion) or pay an *erev Shabbos* visit to a lonely friend.

9. Polish your silver candlesticks and *kiddush* cups on Thursday and set them out on your white Shabbos tablecloth to give yourself and your family a shining greeting on Friday morning. Everyone will feel the spirit of *erev Shabbos* and you can feel like a *balabustah* regardless of the state of the kitchen.

10. Experience can make a difficult task easy. Consult with other homemakers about scheduling, shortcuts and other tips.

The Shabbos Simchah

Sometimes the joy of the Sabbath is further enhanced by a special occasion celebrated with friends and family.

Shalom Zachar: This custom prevails in many Ashkenazi communities. When a boy is born, the first Friday night after his birth is marked by the gathering of well-wishers to enjoy light refreshments after dinner. They join in song and words of Torah, partaking of cakes, fruit and drinks. It is also traditional in some communities to serve chickpeas (*arbes*), eaten by the handful. (See p.76.) You can choose cookies and finger-cakes, or whatever strikes your fancy from the cake and dessert sections.

Kiddush: On Sabbath morning, as on Friday night, after prayer we "make *kiddush*" before partaking of food. This means reciting certain verses, customarily over a cup of wine, which apply to the sanctity of the day. This *kiddush* must be at the table, followed by a meal. But for special occasions we may decide to have a *kiddush*, where cakes and other treats constitute the meal served to our guests before all go home to enjoy their own Shabbos repast. To be a *kiddush*, this spread must include cake or something else (like a noodle-based kugel) on which the *mezonoth* blessing can be recited. Some hostesses serve an assortment of salads and fishes with crackers. A Jerusalem *kiddush* is usually characterized by hot Yerushalmi kugel and pickle spears. (See p.58.) Some even honor their guests with servings of cholent.

The naming of a baby girl, a *bar* or *bas mitzvah*, the calling up to the Torah of a bridegroom (*aufruf*), a new home ... keep looking for occasions! Choosing from among our cakes and cookies, kugels, salads, or other recipes, you should enjoy preparing your *kiddush*. *Mazel tov!*

The Taste of Shabbos

CHALLAH AND WINE:
The Basics

Kiddush is recited over a cup of wine before eating on Friday night, and again before eating the morning meal. The truly industrious may enjoy making their own wine. We have, therefore, included instructions for homemade wine.

Each of the three Sabbath meals is begun with two whole loaves of challah known as *lechem mishneh*. By setting two loaves on the Sabbath table, we recall the manner in which the Creator provided food for our forefathers in the wilderness. Manna fell from heaven each day of the week, sufficient for that day alone, spoiling if kept overnight. But on the sixth day of the week, a double portion fell, and that part saved for the Sabbath retained its freshness. Challah is therefore of great significance in honoring the Sabbath.

CHALLAH

    The mitzvah of "separating *challah*" from dough is the source of the name of our Sabbath bread. Since this mitzvah is considered one of those which are the special province of the Jewish woman, it serves as an added incentive for the homemaker to bake her own challah.

    Challah must be separated from any dough (as opposed to batter) consisting of more than 2 lbs. 13 oz. (1.300 kg.), approximately 10 cups of flour. Similarly, several smaller doughs — raw or baked — that shared the same container (i.e. baking pan, oven tray, even the freezer) and total 2 lbs. 13 oz. (1.300 kg.) have the *challah* requirement. The mitzvah, until the *Beth HaMikdash* (Holy Temple) is rebuilt, calls for the separation of a bit of the dough, bread or cake which is then declared *challah*. When quantities of more than 3 lbs. 12 oz. (1.680 kg.) are involved, it is customary to separate a *kezayith* — ½ oz. (15 gm.) — and the appropriate blessing is recited. The *challah* should be destroyed or disposed of in a dignified manner.

    We have noted in each recipe at what point *challah* should be separated. If one increases or decreases a recipe, one should check above to see if the new volume of flour requires separation of *challah*.

Always Successful Challah

8-9 cups flour
¾-1 cup sugar
1 Tbsp. salt
1-2 oz. (50 gm.) yeast

2½ cups lukewarm water
½ cup oil
¼ cup raisins (optional)
5 eggs

Mix together 2½ cups flour with sugar, salt, yeast (no need to dissolve first), water and oil. Mix in 4 eggs. Beat in 1½ cups flour very well. Add 4-5 cups flour until a very soft dough is formed. Add raisins (optional). Knead. Separate *challah*, if necessary. Let rise 1-2 hours, or refrigerate overnight and then let warm to room temperature for 1-2 hours. Make balls, roll them into ropes and braid. Let rise covered for ½-1 hour. Make egg wash by beating 1 egg. Brush on challah. Bake in preheated oven at 325°F (150°C) for 30 minutes. Apply egg wash once more and bake another 30 minutes at 350°F (175°C). Makes 4 medium-sized challahs.

Sweet Half-and-Half Challah

---

2 oz. (60 gm.) yeast
2 cups warm water
1-1½ cups honey
¾ cup oil

4 eggs
4 cups whole wheat flour
5-6 cups white flour

Mix together yeast, water, honey, oil and eggs. Add the sifted flour. Knead until dough does not stick to fingers. Cover dough with a damp cloth and let rise in a warm place for two hours. Separate *challah*, if necessary. Divide the dough into 6 balls. Divide each ball in three and braid. Let rise for 1 hour. Bake in preheated oven at 350° F (175° C) for 30-45 minutes. Do not overbake. Makes 6 loaves.

Jerusalem Challah

3 oz. (100 gm.) yeast	2 Tbsp. salt
3 eggs	1 cup sugar
1 cup oil	4½ cups warm water
4 lbs. 4 oz. (2 kg.) flour	1 egg yolk

Dissolve yeast in ½ cup warm water, in which 1 Tbsp. sugar and 1 Tbsp. flour have been dissolved. Add 3 eggs, one at a time, sugar, oil and 4 cups water, beating after each addition. Add half the flour, salt, and beat one minute. Mix in the rest of the flour until dough begins to leave side of bowl. For above quantity, separation of *challah* will be necessary. Turn dough onto slightly floured surface. Cover with cloth and allow to rest 10-15 minutes. Knead 10 minutes. Put dough into greased bowl, turning dough until the whole surface is lightly oiled. Cover with a slightly damp, not wet, cloth. Let dough rise until double in bulk, about 2 hours. Punch down. Knead in bowl for 3 minutes. Cover and let rise a second time. Divide into 6 balls. Divide each ball in four. Let dough rest 10 minutes before braiding. Roll into strips. Braid with 4 strips (see illustration). Grease loaf pans. Preheat oven to 350° F (175° C). Brush with egg wash (1 egg yolk plus 1-2 Tbsp. water). Let rise 20-30 minutes before baking. Bake 45 minutes. Makes 6 medium-sized challahs.
Variation: ¾ cup honey may be substituted for sugar.

Save waiting time by letting dough rise in a plastic bag or a very large bowl in the refrigerator overnight. In the morning, remove from refrigerator and let stand half an hour. Then shape and bake.

Rabbi Isaac Luria was accustomed to place twelve challahs on the table at each of the Sabbath meals.

(*Ben Ish Hai*)

Eggless or "Water" Challah

2 oz. (60 gm.) yeast	½ cup oil
9 cups flour	½ cup + 2 tsp. sugar
3 cups water	2 tsp. salt

Dissolve yeast and 2 tsp. sugar in ½ cup warm water. Sift flour into a very large bowl. Make a well in middle of flour. Add 2½ cups water, oil, ½ cup sugar, salt and yeast mixture. Mix until a soft dough is formed. Knead. Separate *challah*, if necessary. Place dough in a greased bowl. Cover with a towel. Let dough rise until double in bulk. Punch down. Knead. Divide into 9 balls. Let dough rest 10 minutes. Roll into ropes and braid into 3 loaves. Let rise 20-30 minutes. Bake at 350° F (175° C) for 45 minutes to 1 hour. Makes 3 challahs.

Knead dough by folding it, pressing it down, turning it, and repeating the procedure. Although the dough is at first slightly sticky, the kneading makes it smooth and elastic.

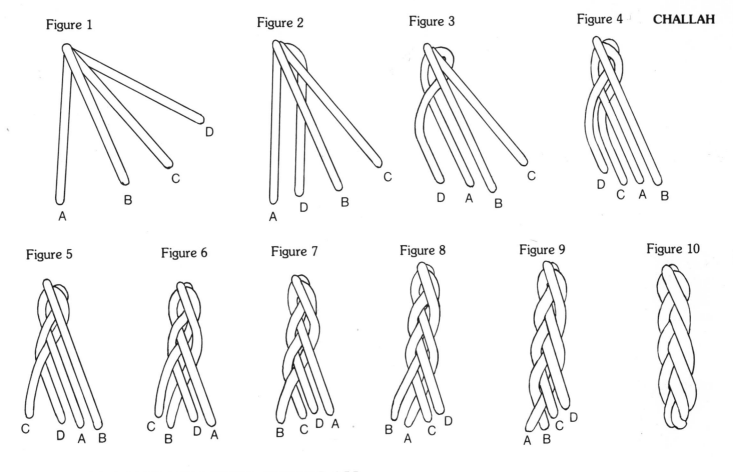

Figure 1 — Figure 2 — Figure 3 — Figure 4 · CHALLAH

Figure 5 — Figure 6 — Figure 7 — Figure 8 — Figure 9 — Figure 10

FOUR-STRAND BRAIDED CHALLAH

Figure 1: Separate and roll dough into 4 equal strands approx. 10 inches long, and pinch together at one end. Place a knife on top of the pinched end to hold it down and allow for easy maneuvering.

Figure 2: Align strands as in Figure 1 and move strand D under strands C and B.

Figure 3: Place D over A.

Figure 4: Move C under B and A.

Figure 5: Place C over D.

Figure 6: Move B under A and D.

Figure 7: Place B over C.

Figure 8: Move A under D and C.

Figure 9: Place A over B.

Figure 10: Continue the under-two, over-one pattern until you reach the end of the strands. Tuck final strand under all and seal.

5

Whole Wheat Challah

2 oz. (60 gm.) yeast	⅓ cup honey
3 cups warm water	2 eggs
1 tsp. sugar	1 Tbsp. salt
10 cups whole wheat flour	poppy, caraway, or sesame seeds
⅓ cup oil	1 egg yolk

The following "sponge method" gives whole wheat challah a lighter texture. Activate yeast in ½ cup water with sugar. Beat in remaining 2½ cups water, 5 cups flour, oil, honey, 2 eggs and salt. Dough should now resemble cake batter. Let rise 30-60 minutes. Punch down. Add the rest of the flour, slowly while kneading, until dough no longer sticks to fingers. Separate *challah*, if necessary. Cover with damp towel. Allow to rise again until double in size. Punch down. Shape into loaves. Place in well-greased loaf pans. Beat egg yolk and brush over loaves. Pat on poppy, caraway or sesame seeds. Let rise for 30 minutes. Bake in preheated oven at 350° F (175° C) for 30 minutes. Makes four medium challahs.

Variation: Substitute 1 cup wheat germ for 1 cup flour and/or 1 cup soy flour for 1 cup flour.

Freezing suggestion: After braiding, place challah on baking sheet without wrapping it and freeze until solid. When hardened, store well-sealed until needed. To bake – thaw unwrapped and let rise at room temperature 4-6 hours. Bake as usual.

When baking challah, place pans on the bottom shelf of the oven so that they don't touch each other or the sides of the oven. The tops of the pans should be level with the middle of the oven.

Pita

The Yemenite tradition is to use pita as challah for *lechem mishneh* (see page 1). (This is not the same kind of pita used for felafel.)

1 oz. (30 gm.) yeast	8 + 1¼ cups flour
3¼ cups water at room temperature	1 Tbsp. salt
1 tsp. sugar	

Dissolve yeast in ¼ cup water. Sprinkle sugar and 1 Tbsp. flour over mixture. Set aside to rise to top of glass. Sift 8 cups (1 kg.) flour into a large bowl. Add salt to flour. Make a well in middle of flour and add yeast mixture. Add 3 cups water. Mix and knead dough. Separate *challah*, if necessary. Let rise until double its original size. Knead dough again and let rise until double in size. Dough should be soft, but not sticky. If dough sticks, dip hands in cold water to facilitate handling. Pinch off pieces of dough to make 12 equal balls. Place balls, one at a time, on a large platter covered with 1¼ cups flour. Dust each ball and knead in flour so that outside of each ball is covered with a very fine layer of flour. With hands, spread out one ball until twice the diameter of original ball. Heat a wide, heavy frying pan with a cover on a medium-low fire. No oil or margarine is used in cooking pita. When frying pan is hot, press and spread pita into pan until it covers entire pan leaving a small margin all around. Cover frying pan. Covering the frying pan is essential to prevent dryness. Turn over the pita after about 5 minutes. Be sure to cover again to cook second side. Remove pita after 5 minutes and place on a dry towel. Continue procedure with each ball of dough. Keep all pitot wrapped in towel or well-sealed plastic bag until use. Makes 12 pitot.

Variation: Middle Eastern or North African pita: After making balls, flatten each into ½" (1.5 cm.) thick circles. Place on a greased cookie sheet, spaced far apart. Prick a few small holes in the middle of each pita with a fork or toothpick. Bake 30-45 minutes at 375° F (185° C).

Allow bread to cool completely on wire rack away from drafts before wrapping or storing.

Leftover challah suggestions:
1) Make a challah kugel for Melaveh Malkah or to freeze for next Shabbos.
2) Make French toast or cinnamon toast.
3) Make fluffy bread-crumbs to keep on hand in the freezer.
4) Prepare croutons for salad or soup and store in tightly-covered tin.

WINE

    Terumoth and *maaseroth* (tithes) should be taken from wine made of grapes grown in *Eretz Yisrael* (the Land of Israel) after the wine-making process has been completed.

    Halachah (Jewish Law) allows that wine may be diluted with water, yet still be classified as *Pri Hagefen* — the fruit of the vine — providing it maintains the taste of common wine. Dilution should be done gradually, up to a maximum of five parts water to one part wine, and one should taste the mixture from time to time to determine that it has not lost the taste of wine. With regard to raisin wine, one should be sure to use no more than five parts water to one part raisins. The raisins must also not be totally dried out.

Homemade Wine

5 quart (5 liter) container   **10 lbs. (5 kg.) wine grapes**
2-3 lbs. (1-1½ kg.) sugar

Grapes should be very ripe (sun-ripened), sweet and juicy. If you want red wine, use at least ¼ deep purple grapes with the green grapes. The greater the proportion of purple grapes, the deeper the color and more mellow the taste of the wine. The grapes must not touch water during the wine-making process. The amount of sugar varies with individual taste. However, making sugarless wine is tricky at best and may result in vinegar. Sugar helps the fermentation process.

(continued)

Method I (Blender Method)

Remove unwashed grapes from stems. Mash in a blender. Pour into vat leaving at least ¼ empty. Add sugar. Close cover loosely. Stir every day for three days. After two months, the wine should be ready to strain.
For straining, you will need:

several (4 or more) large bowls
thin hose or siphon
closely-woven cloth or towel

Stand the vat of wine on a table. Place a big bowl on a chair next to the table. Insert one end of hose into middle of vat, direct other end above bowl. Start to siphon out the wine. If you use a hose, the siphoning can be started by sucking out the air from the bottom of the hose. Once begun, the siphoning should continue until nearly all the wine is removed from vat. The remaining liquid can be strained through a large strainer. These skins and dregs are discarded. Clean and dry vat. Strain wine back into vat through cloth or towel. Keep wine covered loosely for at least 24 hours, then tighten lid. Dilute with ¼-⅓ water before serving.
Serving suggestion: Boil wine, add ⅓ water and cool before serving. The alcohol content will be lower and the taste richer.

With two loaves and with Kiddush, with abundant delicacies and with a generous spirit, those who enjoy the Sabbath will merit much goodness, the coming of the Redeemer, and the World to Come.

(Zemiroth)

Why is Kiddush recited over wine?

Wine is unique in that it becomes special only when it is separated from its source, the grape. Solids are generally considered more physical than liquids. Thus, wine, separated from the solid grape, is more spiritual. Wine, a derivative of the grape, is its essence. When wine enters a physical body, it evokes the spiritual, for it is the result of that process.

(The Bostoner Rebbe)

Part I

Remove unwashed grapes from stems. Put in dry vat, add sugar. Mix well with long-handled spoon or stick. Cover loosely with a cloth. Mix well every few days until sugar has dissolved. Keep loosely covered for 6-8 weeks. Remove contents of vat, a few cupfuls at a time, to a strainer placed in a very large bowl. Save grapes for "raisin wine." Strain the wine a second time through a closely-woven fabric into bottles or a large container. Again, cover loosely (for example, with a piece of paper towel held by an elastic band) as fermentation process continues. Usually the fermentation process stops after about two weeks. At this time, the bottles may be sealed.

Part II "Second Time 'Round" ("Raisin Wine")

Weigh the remaining "used" grapes. Return them to vat, adding 20% sugar and 20% water by weight. Stir occasionally until sugar melts entirely. Keep loosely covered 40 days. Strain through closely-woven fabric.

Whoever sanctifies the Sabbath over wine, lengthens his days in this world and assures himself of a portion in the World to Come.

(Pirkei D'Rabbi Eliezer)

EVENING AND MORNING SABBATH MEALS

The first and second Sabbath meals traditionally feature meat (or poultry) and consist of several courses. We have, therefore, included the various foods we prepare for these two meals in a single large section.

Below is a recommended menu plan, based upon the custom and experience of Jewish homemakers over the years.

Evening meal
    Wine
    Challah
    Fish or other appetizer
    Soup
    Poultry or meat
    Vegetable or other side dish
    Kugel
    One or two salads
    Dessert and/or cake

Morning meal
    Wine
    Challah
    Cold fish or other appetizer
    Cold meat or poultry
    Cholent
    Two salads
    Cold kugel
    Dessert and/or cake

Fish and Other Appetizers

Sabbath dinners are more elaborate than any weekday meal — appropriate treatment for the Sabbath Queen, our honored guest. The Jewish family enjoys lingering round the Sabbath table to savor special Sabbath foods, to share Torah thoughts, and to sing of the Sabbath day in *zemiroth*. Thus, we serve several courses, singing between one and the next.

Fish, in particular, is an essential in Sabbath fare. Folk stories from Jewish communities around the world attest to the great importance always placed on acquiring, at any cost, the best possible fish for the Sabbath.

The hot appetizers in this section are intended for the Friday night meal, while cold ones may be served at any one of the meals.

FISH

This list indicates varieties of kosher fish commonly available in Israel, the United States and Great Britain.

Lean fish:	**Fat fish:**	**In between:**
flounder	salmon	grey mullet (*bourri*)
halibut	mackerel	*kasif*
cod	tuna	
hake (*bakala*)	large carp	
haddock	trout	
pike	whitefish	
small carp	red snapper (*dag adom*)	
sole (*Moshe Rabbenu*)		
amnon		

Lean fish are best fried, steamed, or cooked. Fat fish may be baked, broiled or fried. In Israel, gefilte fish is commonly made from a mixture of two parts silver carp (*kasif*) to one part grey mullet (*bourri*) or two parts *kasif* to one part carp. Sometimes only one fish is used. In the United States, a preferred combination is pike (or pickerel) and whitefish. In England, the mixture is usually equal quantities of haddock and cod.

A Real "Gefilte" (Stuffed) Fish

1 lb. (500 gm.) ground fish	STOCK:
2 whole fish	4 cups water
2 eggs	2 sliced onions
1 large onion, grated	1 carrot
1 carrot, grated	2 sticks celery (optional)
½ cup matzah meal	1 tsp. salt
1 tsp. salt	dash of pepper
⅛ tsp. pepper	1 Tbsp. sugar
¼ cup sugar	
¼-½ cup seltzer or ice water	

Mix ground fish, eggs, onion, carrot, matzah meal, salt, pepper, sugar and seltzer or ice water together very well until firm. Clean whole fish well and slice into 1" slices. Stuff each slice with fish mixture. Chill on a baking tray for at least 4 hours. Drop individual slices into boiling fish stock for 1½-2 hours. Serves 20.

By eating fish on the Sabbath we gain a triple blessing. During Creation, G-d conferred three blessings. On the fifth day fish were blessed, on the sixth day man was blessed, and on the seventh, the Sabbath itself was blessed. Thus, when *fish* is eaten by *man* on the *Sabbath*, he benefits from a three-fold blessing.

(Bnei Yissaschar)

A real time saver: Make a double quantity of gefilte fish mixture and freeze before cooking, either in oblong loaves, or in individual balls. When freezing the balls, first freeze them slightly on a cookie sheet before packaging to prevent them from sticking to one another.

Sweet Gefilte Fish

1 lb. (500 gm.) ground fish or 2 lbs. (1 kg.) whole fish (carp, silver carp or whitefish and pike)	½ cup matzah meal black pepper to taste 4 Tbsp. salt 6 Tbsp. sugar
1 carrot	2 eggs
3 onions	oil

Slice two onions. Sauté in a small amount of oil in frying pan on a small flame until soft and translucent, but not brown. If using whole fish, clean and grind fish. Grind the fried onions. Mix fish well with the onions. Add matzah meal, eggs, 3 Tbsp. sugar, 2 Tbsp. salt and black pepper. Let set 15 minutes. Fill a medium-sized pot half way with water. Add sliced carrot, 1 sliced onion, 2 Tbsp. salt, 3 Tbsp. sugar and black pepper. Bring to a boil. Make fish balls with wet hands, place the balls into the simmering stock. Cook for ¾ hour. When it has cooled, pour the sauce into a jar and refrigerate until it jells. Use as garnish. Serves 15.

Variation: **Spicy Baked Gefilte Fish:** Combine ½ cup tomato sauce, ½ cup water, salt and pepper to taste. Pour over cooked gefilte fish pieces. Bake ½ hour at 350° F (175° C).

Israeli Gefilte Fish

FISH MIXTURE:
1 hard-boiled egg
1 carrot
1 large onion
1 lb. (500 gm.) silver carp
1 lb. (500 gm.) carp (or whitefish
  and pike)
½ cup water
1 raw egg
½ cup matzah meal
½ tsp. salt

3-4 Tbsp. sugar
¼ tsp. pepper

STOCK:
4 cups water
4 carrots
3 onions
1 Tbsp. salt
¾ tsp. pepper
2 Tbsp. sugar
Fish bones and head (optional)

Prepare fish mixture by grinding together hard-boiled egg, carrot and onion. Mix in the fish and regrind the whole combination. Add rest of ingredients. Mix quickly and thoroughly, to get a light and fluffy mixture. In the meantime, prepare stock by bringing water, fish bones and head, carrots, onions and seasonings to a boil in a large pot. Using a large serving spoon to measure, shape fish into balls, flatten out a bit and place into pot of simmering water. Cook covered for 2-2½ hours on low flame. Makes 25 servings.

If you mix fish very well in an electric mixer for about 10 minutes on a medium-high speed, it gets stiff on its own and you need not add the matzah meal (or add just a little bit). Or, refrigerate mixture for 1 hour before shaping into loaves.

Sweet Potato Fish

2 large grey mullet (*bourri*)
  or carp, sliced into 10
  serving pieces
2 carrots
1 sweet potato

6 garlic cloves
4-5 medium onions
½-¾ cup sugar
dash pepper
dash paprika

Salt the fish lightly with coarse salt and let stand for at least 4 hours (or preferably overnight). This will remove the "fishy" taste. Slice onions and carrots into medium-sized pot. Cut sweet potato into quarters and add to pot. Add sugar, spices and garlic. Cover vegetables with water. Cover pot and bring to boil. Add fish and bring to boil again. Reduce heat and simmer for 1½ hours. Cool. Remove fish to deep dish, placing pieces of carrot and sweet potato on or next to each piece. Strain fish sauce and pour over fish pieces. Discard onion slices or use for decoration. The fish sauce jells when refrigerated for a few hours. Serves 10.

In the animal world, fish are the most pure. The flood that destroyed all forms of life in the time of Noah did not destroy the fish, for they alone had remained uncorrupted. Fish require no ritual slaughter or salting before we eat them. They are unaffected by the evil eye. Because of its elevated position among the animal species, fish is deemed proper food for the Jew on the Sabbath.

(Ohr HaShabbos)

Sole Amandine

3 Tbsp. margarine	pepper
3 oz. (100 gm.) blanched, slivered almonds	½ tsp. garlic powder
	1 tsp. paprika
1 lb. (500 gm.) filet of sole	½ cup bread crumbs

Preheat oven to 375°F (185°C). Melt margarine in medium-sized pan. Add almonds and stir until coated, about 2 minutes. Remove almonds and most of margarine from pan. Set aside. Place fish in pan and turn to coat with margarine. Sprinkle top of fish with seasonings, bread crumbs, almonds and margarine. Bake for 20 minutes. Serves 4.

Curried Fish

1 lb. (500 gm.) frozen fish	Any or all of the following
½ tsp. curry powder	(but not more than 2 cups in all):
1 tsp. garlic powder	onions
2 apples	carrots
½ cup raisins	tomatoes
2-4 Tbsp. oil	zucchini
salt to taste	corn
	string beans
	mushrooms

Preheat oven to 350° F (175° C) and bake fish until done. In the meantime, dice and stir-fry the vegetables and fruit in a small amount of oil. Sprinkle with curry powder, garlic powder and salt. Pour over cooled fish. Serve hot or cold. Serves 5.

Baked Fish in Russian Dressing

½ cup ketchup	2 lbs. (1 kg.) fish filets
½ cup mayonnaise	

Preheat oven to 350° F (175° C). Combine ketchup and mayonnaise. Place fish in baking dish. Spread with ketchup-mayonnaise mixture. If you wish you can layer fish and dressing. Bake for ½ hour. Serve warm. Serves 8.

Yosef Mokir Shabbos, who held the Sabbath in high esteem, lived near a very wealthy gentile. Soothsayers had told the man that all his tremendous wealth would be consumed by Yosef Mokir Shabbos. Seeking to prevent this, he sold all his possessions and purchased instead a precious jewel which he always kept in his hat.

One day as he was crossing a bridge, the wind blew his hat off and the jewel fell into the water where it was swallowed up by a big fish. The fish was caught and brought to market late Friday afternoon. People wondered who would want to buy such an expensive fish at such a late hour. Then someone said, "Bring the fish to Yosef Mokir Shabbos! He will not refuse

Moroccan Fish

2 onions, finely chopped
oil
3 tomatoes, finely chopped
1 Tbsp. turmeric
salt
pepper
juice of ½ lemon

6 hake (*bakala*) filets
dash sweet paprika
2 crushed garlic cloves
 or 1 Tbsp. garlic powder (optional)
chili powder (optional), or chili pepper
 (optional)
olives (optional)

Place onions in pan with a little oil and fry over low flame until soft. Add tomatoes, cover and simmer for a few minutes. Add spices and lemon juice. Place fish on top, sprinkle with paprika and baste with onion-tomato-spice mixture. Cover and cook over low flame for ½ hour. Garnish with olives. Serves 6.

Israeli Broiled Fish

4 lbs. (2 kg.) grey
 mullet (*bourri*)

4 sweet red peppers
8 garlic cloves

Clean fish and slice in serving pieces. Puree peppers and garlic cloves in blender. Spread over fish. Broil 20-30 minutes, until browned. Serve warm or cold. Serves 6.

Sweet and Sour Fish

3 lbs. (1¼ kg.) striped bass
2 medium onions, coarsely chopped
1 carrot, sliced
1 tsp. salt
⅛ tsp. pepper

1½ tsp. mixed pickling spices
2 bay leaves
⅓ cup sugar
3-4 slices lemon and/or
 ½ cup vinegar

Cook onions, carrots, salt, pepper, spices, bay leaves, sugar and lemon in 4 cups water. Boil and simmer covered ¼ hour. Add vinegar. Arrange fish on top and simmer covered for 1 hour, basting occasionally. Remove lemon slices. Cool and refrigerate.

such a fish in honor of the Sabbath."

The fishermen brought him the fish and he bought it happily. As he was cutting it open, he found the precious jewel. He later sold the jewel for a vast sum of money and was able to honor the Sabbath with sumptuous dishes and fine wine for the rest of his life.

A wise man remarked about him: "He who extends himself for the Sabbath, will be repaid by the Sabbath."

(Talmud Bavli)

To remove fish odors from pots, pans, and hands, rub with a cut lemon or some salt, then rinse.

Stuffed Cabbage

12-16 cabbage leaves	SAUCE:
FILLING:	1 Tbsp. oil
1½ lbs. (¾ kg.) ground beef	1 small onion, chopped fine
1 small onion, diced	1 peeled apple, shredded
dash pepper	1½ cups tomato juice
dash sugar	2 cups tomato puree
¼ cup raw rice	2 tsp. lemon juice
1 egg	4-8 Tbsp. brown sugar
	¼ cup raisins

Check cabbage leaves for insects. Combine filling ingredients and divide among the leaves. Roll each one, tucking sides in firmly. Meanwhile saute onions and apples in oil till soft. Add remaining sauce ingredients, heat and add cabbage rolls. Simmer for about two hours, occasionally spooning sauce over rolls.

Sweet and Sour Meatballs

MEATBALLS:	SAUCE:
½ cup hot water	1 cup cold water
1 heaping Tbsp. bread crumbs	½ cup ketchup
1 lb. (500 gm.) ground meat	3 Tbsp. sugar
1 onion, chopped	1 slice of lemon
2 eggs	¼ cup raisins
pinch salt	1 Tbsp. margarine
pinch pepper	1 Tbsp. cornstarch dissolved in
	1 Tbsp. water

Pour hot water over bread crumbs. Mix with meat, onion, eggs and seasonings. Form meatballs. Combine sauce ingredients in 2½ quart pot and bring to a boil, stirring. Add meatballs and simmer ½ hour. Makes 6 servings.

A note about liver:

While most kosher meat and fowl sold today has already been "made kosher" by salting, the kashering of liver over the flame is left up to the housewife. Liver — from beef or poultry — must be rinsed, freed of membrane endings, salted lightly, and broiled in a grating over an open flame, until done. Once done, the liver should be rinsed immediately and the grating itself kashered over the flame.

Recipes which require cooking the liver after broiling it, are intended for liver broiled within three days of slaughter. For clarification, please consult your rabbinic authority.

words" — to teach that your Sabbath speech must differ from your weekday speech.

(Talmud Bavli)

Chopped Liver

2 lbs. (1 kg.) liver	**small piece of challah**
2-5 medium onions	**salt**
2-5 eggs	**pepper**

Kasher liver and divide into 4 packages. Freeze individually until ready for use. Each package serves about 6 people as an appetizer. Quantity of eggs and onions varies with individual taste and budget. Sauté onions, stirring often, until lightly browned. (Very dark brown loses the juiciness and becomes bitter.) Hardboil the eggs. Grind one portion of liver, eggs and then onions. Grind challah last to clean out grinder. Mix thoroughly, mashing with back of spoon, until color is uniform. Add salt and pepper to taste.

Even a four year old can set a proper table if you draw a picture of a place-setting to serve as a guide.

Chicken Livers in Mushroom Sauce

1 lb. (500 gm.) chicken livers	**2 cups cooked rice or bow noodles**
1½ cups mushroom sauce	

Kasher chicken livers. Prepare mushroom sauce from packaged mix or see p. 23. Add livers, cut into bite-size pieces, to sauce. (At this point, mixture may be frozen or refrigerated.) Just before Shabbos, reheat mixture and prepare rice or noodles. Keep warm. Serve livers on a bed of rice or noodles. Serves 6.

Chicken Liver Entrée

10 chicken livers	**6-8 eggs**
2 large onions	

Kasher livers. Cut into small pieces. Dice and brown onions in a small amount of oil. Add livers to browned onions. Boil eggs. Serve eggs cut in halves with a large tablespoon of liver-onion mixture. Add more onions to taste. Serves 6-8.

An interesting way to serve appetizers is in toast cups. Trim crust from bread. Brush with melted margarine. Press into muffin tins and toast in a moderate oven for a few minutes.

Meat Blintzes

LEAVES:	FILLING:
1 cup flour	**2 cups leftover meat, chicken**
1 cup water	**or turkey (free of bones and skin)**
3 eggs	**1 onion, chopped and browned in**
pinch salt	**1 Tbsp. oil**
	1 egg

It is a Yemenite tradition to begin a meal with Jaale. All invited guests and the host family prepare varieties of dried fruit (raisins, dates, figs, apricots, apples) roasted nuts, peanuts, sunflower seeds, pumpkin seeds and fresh fruit cut into serving pieces. Bowls of these are passed from the oldest to the youngest along with liqueurs and other beverages.

Combine ingredients for leaves until mixture is smooth. Pour a thin layer into a heated crêpe pan or 8″ frying pan. When leaf starts to leave sides of pan, turn it carefully and bake for two seconds on reverse side. Turn onto a plate and repeat until batter is used up. This makes 12 leaves. Prepare filling by grinding or chopping finely meat and onion. Add egg. Place one-twelfth on each leaf. Turn in sides and roll, forming blintzes. Fry in oil and serve one on each appetizer plate with mushroom or tomato sauce. Serves 12.

Egg Rolls

PANCAKES:
2 eggs
½ cup water
½ tsp. salt
½ cup sifted flour
1 Tbsp. oil

FILLING:
1 cup sliced celery

½ cup sliced onions
1 cup Chinese or white
cabbage or bean sprouts
2 Tbsp. oil
1½ tsp. salt
¼ tsp. pepper
½ cup flaked tuna or
sliced chicken (optional)

Beat the eggs, water and salt together. Beat in the flour. Heat a 7-inch skillet with a little oil and pour a little of the batter into it to make a thin pancake. Cook until browned on the bottom. Remove, browned side up, and stack while preparing the filling. It is not necessary to oil skillet after each pancake. Cook the celery, onions and carefully checked cabbage or sprouts in the oil for 5 minutes, stirring frequently. Stir in the salt, pepper and tuna or chicken. Cool. Place a heaping tablespoon of the filling at one end of each pancake and roll up, tucking opposite end in. Seal with a little beaten egg and chill. Fry in deep fat heated to 380° F (190° C) until browned. Serve with mushroom sauce (see below). Serves 5.

Mushroom Sauce

3 Tbsp. margarine
1 cup fresh mushrooms, sliced
or ½ cup canned, drained
3 Tbsp. flour
onion salt or onion juice (optional)

¼ tsp. salt
dash pepper
1½ cups water
1 tsp. soy sauce

Melt margarine in saucepan, sauté mushrooms until liquid evaporates. (If canned, stir into margarine, sautéing briefly.) Stir in flour, adding seasonings. Then add water and soy sauce, gradually, stirring and cooking until thickened.
Variation: Sauté one onion, diced, in the margarine before adding mushrooms.

The story is told of the little boy who came home from *cheder* crying. "What has happened?" asked his mother. "The rebbe asked us a question that I could not understand," answered the young boy, "He asked me again and again, but I don't understand the question at all." "Tell me what the rebbe asked," urged his mother. "He asked us what the law would be for a man who has become lost in a desert and doesn't know what day it is. He wanted us to tell him on which day such a man should observe Shabbos!" "What don't you understand, my son?" "How could it be?" asked the boy in incredulity and frustration. "How could he not know which day is Shabbos? The air is different, the light is different, there is a special smell, a special feel... What is the question?"

Chicken a la King

4 Tbsp. margarine	1 cup canned mushrooms
4 Tbs. flour	¾ cup slivered almonds (optional)
2½ cups chicken broth	1 cup green peas (optional)
1 egg yolk	3 cups diced cooked chicken
1/3 cup sweet red pepper, cut small	

In 2½ quart pot, melt margarine. Add flour and stir. Add chicken broth (which may be made by adding powdered mix to boiling water) to pot and stir until mixture boils. Blend 2 Tbsp. of the hot sauce into egg yolk in a dish and add to liquid in pot. Stir until thick. Add remaining ingredients. Heat, but do not allow to boil. Serve in pastry shells, or on mashed potatoes or rice. Do not freeze this mixture. Serves 8-10.

Vegetarian Liver

5 large onions, sliced	½ cup walnuts, ground
3-4 Tbsp. oil	salt, to taste
½ cup string beans or peas, fresh, frozen or canned	pepper, to taste
4 hard boiled eggs	water

Over low heat, sauté onions in oil slowly until uniformly dark (about 1½ hours). Then add string beans and water to cover. Cook until water has evaporated. Beans should be soft. Remove from heat, add other ingredients and chop finely. Refrigerate overnight. Serve cold. Serves 4-6.

Egg Onion Salad

8 eggs	1½ tsp. salt
1 onion	½ tsp. pepper
2 Tbsp. oil	

Boil eggs until hard. Cool, peel and grate. Grate onion and mix with egg. Add oil, salt and pepper to taste. Serves 4-6.
Variation: Dice and sauté onions before mixing with egg.

One of Jerusalem's renowned *balabustes* tells the following about her first attempts at "making Shabbos." Far from family, newly arrived in Jerusalem, she consulted a wise older woman for advice on how to prepare for the special day. The experienced homemaker gave her recipes, menu plans and suggestions till her head fairly spun. The younger woman was close to tears, when her mentor smiled comfortingly: "Don't worry, just make each thing 'lekovod Shabbos (in honor of the Sabbath). It will have to be good!". There was such certainty in her voice that the bride went home reassured. To this day, she has found no better advice. All that she prepares 'lekovod Shabbos,' is guaranteed success.

P'tcha

25-30 chicken feet	pepper
6 giblets	onion powder
1 large onion	garlic powder
salt	5-7 hard-boiled eggs (optional)

Scald chicken feet in boiling water. Peel off yellow outer skin. Place whole onion, chicken feet and giblets in a saucepan. Cover with water. Bring to a boil in covered pot, adding only a drop of salt. Simmer, adding water when necessary for 3½ hours. Remove giblets and feet immediately. Debone feet, discarding only bone. Chop well all remaining material. Pour liquid from pot into flat pan (up to 1½″ deep). Add chopped giblets and feet, plus lots of garlic powder, onion powder and pepper to taste. (This is a spicy dish.) Stir a little. Cool it in refrigerator. As it starts to jell, add sliced egg on top. When cold, cut in squares and serve with mustard.

Homemade Shmaltz & Greben (Chicken Fat & Cracklings)

poultry fat and skins	diced onions
salt	

Cut the fat and skins into 1″ pieces. Combine all ingredients and add water to cover. Cook on low heat so fat melts and cracklings do not burn. Remove cracklings when brown and use in chopped liver. Drain the shmaltz to add to any meat dish for extra taste.

Why do we eat p'tcha on the Sabbath? Falsehood has no leg to stand on, whereas the truth can stand on its own. The Sabbath bears witness to Creation. It is a sign of truth. We therefore eat a delicacy made from feet on the Sabbath day!
(Ohr HaShabbos)

Cleaning the range very well before covering it for Shabbos saves dismay and hard work after Shabbos ends. (The intense covered heat burns on every spill.)

Soups and Soup Accompaniments

Soup is a common feature of the Friday night meal in most Jewish communities. For many, chicken soup is the *sine qua non*. Others prefer to rotate their favorite soup recipes.

In some communities which existed for generations (or still do) in extremely hot climates, soup does not play a role at all in the Sabbath menu, but is replaced by salads or hors d'oeuvres. For others, like the Jews of Yemen, the soup course is expanded to include virtually the entire meal.

Suggestions for soup chicken

1. Sprinkle salt and garlic powder on chicken pieces after removing from soup and fry or broil for a few minutes.
2. Dice and sauté 1 tomato, 2 stalks celery, 1 onion and 1 green pepper. Add chicken pieces after removing from soup and braise lightly. Serve on a bed of rice.
3. Remove skin and bones. Grind for use in "meat" blintzes, knishes or kreplach.
4. Use chicken for salad, see p. 41.

Old Jerusalem Chicken Soup

¾ cup white beans
2 zucchini
2 carrots
2 potatoes

2 onions
2 tomatoes
1 chicken, cut into serving
   pieces

Soak beans 6-12 hours. Check carefully. Cut zucchini, carrots and potatoes into large pieces. Put all the vegetables and the beans into a large pot. Place the chicken pieces on top, cover with water, bring to a boil and simmer 2-3 hours. Take out the tomatoes before serving. Add kneidlach or kugelach. Serves 6.

Yemenite Soup

1 chicken, cut into
   serving portions or 2 lbs (1 kg.)
   meat, cubed
5 medium carrots
5 medium onions
5 medium potatoes

1 squash
1 tomato
2 celery stalks
2 Tbsp. hawaich (Yemenite spice
   mixture) or 2 tsp. curry powder +
   1 tsp. pepper + 2 tsp. paprika

Boil water in a large pot. Add chicken or meat pieces. Skim off brown foam with spoon. When soup is clear, add vegetables and *hawaich* (a traditional Yemenite spice, which gives this soup its characteristic deep yellow color). Simmer chicken soup for 1 hour on a low flame. Meat soup should simmer 3-4 hours. Meat and vegetables are served togther in a soup bowl. Served with pita, this soup is the traditional Friday night meal of many Yemenite families. Serves 5.

Chicken Soup

1 whole chicken	1 onion
2 carrots	salt
3 stalks celery	pepper
1 Tbsp. chicken soup powder (optional)	

Clean chicken and cut into pieces. Cover with water (8-10 cups). Bring all ingredients to a boil, then simmer for 2 hours. Cool. Take out chicken pieces to serve separately. Strain soup. Serves 6.

For clear soup, strain through a closely-woven cloth, before Shabbos.

Shurba

This Syrian soup is served in the morning.

1 chicken breast	salt to taste
¾ cup rice	soup powder to taste

Boil large potful (at least 4 cups) of water and add all ingredients. Cook ½ hour on high flame and put on covered low fire overnight. This is a thick, rich soup, perfect for a winter Shabbat day. The chicken comes out very moist.
Variation: Add ½ cup white beans with rice. Season with turmeric and cumin.

Skim soup when cool by patting surface with a paper towel or refrigerate and remove congealed fat with a spoon.

Favorite Tomato Soup

6 cups water	Beef bones
3 cups tomato purée	1 lb. (500 gm.) flanken or chuck
½ tsp. sour salt (lemon salt)	½ tsp. pepper
1 Tbsp. garlic powder	2-3 medium whole onions
1 Tbsp. coarse salt	¼ cup sugar, to taste

Put all ingredients, except sugar, into a large pot. Cover and simmer over a low flame. When simmering, add sugar. Stir occasionally and remove onions when soft. The longer this soup cooks and the more often reheated, the better it tastes. Freezes well.

The Sabbath appeared before the Lord with a complaint: "Master of the Universe! Every day of the week has its mate, and I have none." The Lord replied: "The people of Israel will be your mate."

(Midrash)

Thick Tomato Soup

1 large onion, chopped
2 celery stalks, chopped
2 Tbsps. margarine
4-5 cups boiling water
2 lbs. (1 kg.) ripe tomatoes

¼ cup brown rice
1 potato, grated
salt
pepper
garlic powder

Sauté onion and celery in margarine until soft. Pour boiling water over tomatoes to skin, saving water for soup. Skin tomatoes and slice. Add all ingredients except for potato. Cook until rice is almost tender. Add grated potato and continue cooking 15 more minutes. Serves 4-6.

Variation: Save rice to add with grated potato. Cook other ingredients about half an hour. Then purée entire mixture in blender. Pour back into pot and add rice and grated potato. Cook half an hour or more.

Once the Emperor of Rome questioned Rabbi Yehoshua ben Chananiah, "Why does the Sabbath food smell so delicious?" "We have a special spice, called "Shabbos" that we put into the dishes that makes them so appetizing," was Rabbi Yehoshua's reply.

(Talmud Bavli)

Vegetable Soup

2 Tbsp. oil
1 large onion, sliced
4 medium carrots
4 potatoes
4 squash

string beans, cooked chick peas,
   peeled tomatoes, pumpkin (optional)
½-1 cup oatmeal
water
salt
pepper

Sauté onion in oil until transparent. Cut carrots, potatoes and squash into chunks. Add remaining ingredients and enough water to cover plus 3 cups. Season to taste. Cook soup for 1 hour. The oatmeal in this recipe disappears leaving the soup nice and thick. Serves 6-8.

Variation: Pour into blender or food processor and blend until just chunky or smooth, as desired.

If soup is too salty, a few raw potatoes can be added to absorb most of the salt.

Thick Vegetable Soup

1 cup split peas
½ cup pearl barley
1 cup chopped cabbage
1 cup chopped celery
½ cup chopped onions

4 diced or grated carrots
3 diced or grated squash
2 diced or grated potatoes
salt to taste
pepper to taste

Check peas, barley and cabbage (cabbage leaves should be checked prior to chopping). If possible, soak peas and barley overnight, or for a few hours. Put all vegetables in a large pot. Add water to cover vegetables plus 2 cups more. Bring to a quick boil. Lower flame and simmer for 1½ hours on a medium flame. You may want to blend about half the amount to thicken it. Serves 12.

Like tears, beads of perspiration that fall during the course of Sabbath preparations also possess the power to erase our transgressions. Thus, working hard in honor of the Sabbath is valuable indeed.

(Ari , *Sha'arei Teshuva*)

Split Pea Soup

¾ cup green split peas
½ cup pearl barley
2 diced carrots
1 large stalk celery

1 diced onion
salt
2 squash (optional)

Wash split peas and check. (Soaking in water will shorten cooking time.) Combine all ingredients and add enough water to cover. Add salt. Cook over a low flame for 1½-2 hours, stirring frequently. Serves 6.
Variation: Put in food processor and then add bite-size pieces frankfurters.
Optional accompaniments: croutons, bean sprouts, roasted ground almonds.

"If I safeguard the Sabbath, then G-d will safeguard me. It is a sign forever and ever between Him and me."

(Zemiroth)

Onion Soup

5 cups thinly sliced onions
2 small cloves garlic (optional)
1 Tbsp. oil
1 Tbsp. soy sauce
3 Tbsp. dry white wine

½ tsp. mustard powder
1-2 tsp. salt
few dashes white pepper
pinch sugar
6 cups water

Cook onions and garlic in small amount of oil, until light brown. Add remaining ingredients. Cook slowly, covered, at least 30 minutes. Serves 6.

Minestrone Soup

1 cup small white beans   handful of fresh parsley
2 Tbsp. olive oil   6 tomatoes, peeled
1 onion, diced   2 cups shredded cabbage
1 cup celery, diced   1 Tbsp. salt
1 clove garlic, minced   2 Tbsp. tomato paste
2 quarts water   ½ cup small macaroni

Soak beans overnight and check. Heat oil. Sauté onion, celery and garlic. Add rest of ingredients except salt, tomato paste and macaroni. Simmer 2-3 hours. Add salt, tomato paste and macaroni and cook another 15 minutes, until macaroni is done. Serves 6-8.

ACCOMPANIMENTS:

Homemade Farfel

1½ cups flour   1 Tbsp. cold water
2 eggs   ½ tsp. salt

Knead all ingredients well and form a ball. Let the ball of dough dry 30-60 minutes. Grate coarsely and spread pieces out on a towel to dry. For darker color, toast on a flat baking sheet 5 minutes in a medium oven, turning pieces over. Farfel keeps for months in a dry place. Boil in soup as a garnish.

Soup Nuts

3 eggs, slightly beaten   1 tsp. salt
2 Tbsp. oil   2 cups flour, approximately

Mix ingredients, adding enough flour so that dough can be rolled into pencil-thin rolls. Form three or four of these. Cut each into ½" pieces. Bake in well-greased pans at 375°F (185°C), about 20 minutes. When cold, store in covered containers.

Two angels of the L-rd accompany every man as he returns home from prayer on Friday night — one is good, the other bad. When he enters his home to find the candles burning, the table set, and his bed freshly made, the good angel speaks: "May it be the will of G-d that next Sabbath will be the same," and the bad angel is forced to reply: "Amen!" But if he finds none of these things, the bad angel speaks: "May it be the will of G-d that next Sabbath will be the same," and the good angel is forced to reply "Amen!"

(Talmud Bavli)

Kreplach

DOUGH:	FILLING:
2 cups flour	**3 cups leftover cooked meat**
2 eggs	**1 raw onion**
1-2 Tbsp. water	**1 egg**
1 tsp. oil	

Combine dough ingredients. With oiled hands, knead for a minute or two. Roll out dough on a floured board. Cut into circles. Put meat and onion through a grinder. Add egg. Place 1 Tbsp. of filling in each circle. Fold circles in half, and with wet fingers pinch closed, being careful not to leave any openings. Drop into boiling soup or salted water. Boil for 30 minutes. May be drained and frozen in single layers, then transferred to plastic bags. Makes about 20-40 kreplach.
Variations: Fill kreplach with chopped liver (pg. 21) or potato filling (pg. 77).

If your plans to devote a few minutes each day to each child aren't working out too well – take advantage of the unique spirit and pace of Shabbos. Just a short period of learning something together – you and your child – can be uplifting for both.

Matzah Balls (Kneidlach)

1 cup coarse matzah meal	**salt**
½ cup water	**pepper**
4 beaten eggs	**garlic powder (optional)**
⅓ cup oil	

Mix all ingredients together well. Refrigerate at least one hour. Wet hands, form balls and drop into rapidly boiling soup, or salted water. Cook for 20 minutes. After cooking and cooling, matzah balls can be drained and frozen. Boil again for 15 minutes before serving. Makes 12-20 kneidlach, depending on size.

Croûtons

Remove crusts from day-old bread. Cut into small cubes. Heat oil in a skillet, throw in bread cubes, frying till evenly golden. Bread cubes may also be browned on a baking sheet in a hot oven at 400° F. (200° C) for 10-15 minutes.

Kugelach

2 eggs	2 tsp. water
2 tsp. salt	1 cup flour

Beat eggs, salt and water. Add flour until smooth batter is formed. Fry by spoonfuls in hot oil until light brown. Turn over and fry on other side.

Egg Drop for Soup

1 egg, beaten	3 Tbsp. flour
dash of salt	¼ cup cold water

Stir all ingredients together until smooth. Drop slowly from end of spoon into boiling soup. Cook five minutes.

One should enjoy the Sabbath by eating, drinking and resting — the more, the better. Even if one cannot be certain that his enjoyment is for the sake of fulfilling G-d's will, the very pleasure that he derives from the Sabbath is a great mitzvah itself, beyond measure... .

(Rabbi Levi Yitzchak of Berditchov)

Poultry and Meat

The Jew spares no expense to honor the Sabbath Queen with the finest foods possible. Thus, world over, the first two Sabbath meals usually feature meat or poultry as the main dish.

Indeed, the refrain of a popular Friday night *zemer* asserts that we "indulge in delights: fatted fowl, quail, and fish."

Unable to locate a tempting quail recipe, we have nonetheless gathered a rich array of meaty main dishes — each one a Sabbath delight.

Pollo Encebollado a la Aragonesa
(Aragon Chicken)

3-4 lb. (1½-2 kg.) chicken, cut
   into pieces
flour
oil
2 onions, finely chopped

salt
pepper
1 tsp. cinnamon
½ tsp. ground cloves
½ cup dry white wine

Coat pieces of chicken with flour. Brown in oil in frying pan. Cover chicken with the chopped onion. Add salt, pepper, cinnamon and ground cloves. Cover the frying pan, reduce flame to low and simmer until onions are transparent. Add white wine. Simmer until chicken is tender. Serve piping hot on bed of rice.

Chicken with Green Beans Sephardic Style

3-4 lb. (1½-2 kg.) chicken, cut
   into pieces
2 lb. (1 kg.) green beans
2 onions, finely chopped
2 Tbsp. oil
juice of 1 lemon

½ tsp. cinnamon
¼ tsp. nutmeg
salt
pepper
2-3 Tbsp. tomato paste
hot cooked rice (optional)

Remove ends of beans. Cut the beans into halves or thirds. Sauté onions in oil until transparent. Add chicken and brown on all sides. Add beans, cook lightly until soft. Add lemon juice and spices. Stir in tomato paste. Add 1-2 Tbsp. or more water as necessary to prevent burning. Cover pot. Simmer on lowest flame until tender. Serve piping hot on bed of rice.

Once upon a time, a prince was captured by his father's enemies. After a long time, he received a secret message from his father, the king, encouraging him not to give up hope, and to retain his princely manner, even in the midst of the wolves of prey among whom he was forced to live, for he would soon attain his release, either through war or by peaceful means.

The prince was overjoyed and wished to celebrate, but could not, of course, reveal the secret. What did he do? He invited his lowly companions to the local inn, and ordered drinks for everyone. They celebrated because of the wine and liquor, while he celebrated because of his father's letter.

Similarly, on Shabbos, our bodies feast with the good food and drink we serve it, but our souls celebrate the opportunity to be close to our Creator.

(*Toldot Ya'akov Yosef*)

Tangy Roast Chicken

1 chicken	2 Tbsp. brown sugar
4 big onions, sliced	¼ cup ketchup
2 Tbsp. oil	2 Tbsp. soy sauce
½ cup water	

Roast chicken uncovered for 1 hour at 350° F (175° C). Sauté onions. Add water, brown sugar, ketchup and soy sauce. Pour over chicken, cover and bake additional ½ hour or more. Serve hot or cold.

Baked Chicken with an Assortment of Sauces

Cut chicken into quarters or smaller pieces (Some cooks remove the skin.) Sprinkle each piece lightly with paprika, or garlic powder and/or black pepper. (Do *not* salt.)

Arrange pieces in a single layer in a roasting pan. Then choose a sauce from the selections below, following the directions carefully.

Amounts are intended for two medium-sized chickens.

All are baked (covered or uncovered as per instructions) at 350° F (175° C) and are done when brown and fork-tender. Chicken prepared this way can be served hot at the evening meal and cold at the morning meal.

Honey-Garlic Sauce
Combine:

6 Tbsp. honey	1 tsp. garlic powder
6 Tbsp. soy sauce	1 tsp. ginger

Coat chicken pieces with mixture; bake uncovered, basting often for 1 hour.

A l'Orange
Combine:

2 onions, sliced and fried in oil	1 tsp. black pepper
2 tsp. paprika	juice of 2 oranges

Pour over chicken pieces. Bake uncovered for 45 minutes or longer, basting often.

Coffee Sauce

Combine:

¾ cup strong hot coffee
(about 1 Tbsp. instant coffee
to ¾ cup boiling water)
⅓ cup ketchup
3 Tbsp. soy sauce

2 Tbsp. lemon juice
2 Tbsp. wine vinegar
(or other vinegar)
1 Tbsp. oil
¼ cup brown sugar

Pour over chicken and cover pan for first ½ hour. Baste and continue baking for another ½ hour, uncovered.

Apricot Sauce

Combine:

½ cup apricot jam
½ cup mayonnaise

½ tsp. black pepper
1 tsp. garlic powder

Spread on chicken pieces. Bake for 45 minutes covered, then for about ½ hour uncovered.

Barbecue Sauce

Combine:

1 cup canned tomato sauce
1 medium onion, chopped
1 clove garlic, minced
¼ cup soy sauce

2 Tbsp. sugar
1 tsp. mustard
⅛ tsp. paprika

Pour over chicken and bake uncovered for about 1 hour, basting occasionally.

Mushroom Chicken

3-4 lb. (1½-2 kg.) chicken, cut
into pieces
dash of pepper
garlic powder
1 (heaping) Tbsp. mushroom soup mix

1 (heaping) Tbsp. chicken soup mix
1 cup water
1 cup white wine
½ lb. (250 gm.) fresh mushrooms
or 1 8-oz (250 gm.) can

Sprinkle garlic powder liberally over chicken pieces. Combine rest of ingredients for sauce. Add chicken and simmer in a covered pot for 1-1½ hours until chicken is tender. Serve hot.

Rabbi Yochanan said in the name of Rabbi Shimon bar Yochai: If Israel were to observe but two Sabbaths in accordance with the law, they would immediately be redeemed!

(Talmud Bavli)

The L-rd said to Israel: If you succeed in observing the Sabbath, I will consider it as though you have kept all the commandments in the Torah.

(Midrash Rabbah)

Fricassée

oil	1 tsp. paprika
1 large onion, chopped	1 lb. (500 gm.) ground beef
2 stalks celery, diced	1 small onion, grated
½ lb. (250 gm.) chicken gizzards	1 egg beaten
½ lb. (250 gm.) wings and necks	2-3 Tbsp. matzah meal or bread crumbs

In a large pot sauté onion and celery in oil until soft, but not brown. Wash gizzards and remove fat. Cut into small pieces. Add to pot with 4 cups of water. Simmer covered for 1 hour. Add wings, necks and paprika. Make small meatballs combining ground meat, onion, egg and matzah meal or bread crumbs. Add to pot. Cook 1 hour longer.

The amount of poultry used in a prepared recipe may be doubled without altering amounts of sauce ingredients. The juices released by the chicken will add enough extra liquid.

Netanya Chicken with Rice

1 chicken, cut into pieces	2 cups water
1 cup tomato paste	2 Tbsp. honey
	cooked rice

Place chicken in deep pot. Mix tomato paste, water and honey and pour over chicken. Cook for 1 hour or until tender. Serve each chicken piece on a bed of warm rice. Pour sauce over each serving.

Shabbat in a Pot

oil to cover pan	1 cup brown rice
1 onion, diced	1 chicken cut in serving pieces
1 carrot diced	¼ cup tomato paste
1 zucchini, diced	1¾ cup water
3-5 cloves garlic, minced	1 Tbsp. soy sauce
sesame seeds (optional)	salt to taste

In a large frying pan, sauté onion, carrot, zucchini, garlic and sesame seeds in oil till soft. Add rice. Place chicken on top of rice mixture and pour liquid over it. Bring to the boil and cover. Lower heat. Simmer about 45 minutes or until liquid is absorbed. With soup and salad, you have a complete meal. The rice takes on the flavor of the chicken. Delicious! Serves 4.

"Six days shall you labor and do all your work". (Exodus 20) When the Sabbath enters we should feel as if all our work is complete, our minds and bodies free.

(Midrash)

38

Pot-Roasted Chicken with Olives (Gourmet Oriental Dish)

1 3 lb. (1½ kg.) chicken, cut
  into pieces
2 Tbsp. oil
2 medium onions, chopped
2 cloves garlic, chopped
1 fresh or pickled medium sweet
  pepper, chopped

2 tomatoes, sliced
12 pitted olives
1 cup white rice
1 cup dry white wine
1 lb. (500 gm.) frozen peas

Brown chicken in hot oil in large skillet, then remove to platter. Place onions, garlic, pepper, tomatoes, olives, rice and wine into skillet and stir. Arrange chicken on top and cover. Simmer for at least 40 minutes until chicken is tender. Check seasonings. Add peas. Simmer 5-10 minutes more. Serve piping hot.

Clean chickens easily by immersing in boiling water for 1-2 minutes, or by pouring boiling water over them.

Polynesian Chicken

8 chicken quarters
1 tsp. garlic powder
1 tsp. paprika
3 Tbsp. French dressing (or substitute
  mixture of ketchup and mayonnaise)
1 can pineapple chunks with liquid

1 can water chestnuts with liquid
1 Tbsp. soy sauce
1 Tbsp. lemon juice
2 Tbsp. cornstarch
½ cup chicken soup
1 cup cooked stringbeans

Heat oven to 450° F (225° C). Sprinkle chicken pieces with garlic powder and paprika and brush top of each piece with dressing. Place skin side down in large roaster and roast 15 minutes. Remove pineapple chunks and water chestnuts from their liquid. Set aside, in a bowl. Combine liquids. Mix in soy sauce, lemon juice mixed with cornstarch and chicken soup. Pour this over the chicken pieces. Turn pieces over, skin side up, and return to oven uncovered, for 40 minutes. Add cooked stringbeans to the pineapple and water chestnuts. Toss well. Before Shabbos, heat pineapple, water chestnuts and cooked stringbeans and place on warm part of covered flame (blech). Do not let it cook. Also before Shabbos, reheat chicken and sauce in a hot oven. At serving time, place chicken pieces on platter, pour pineapple-chestnut-stringbean mixture over chicken, and pour sauce over all. Serve with rice.

"Do not kindle a fire on the Sabbath". (Exodus 35) The Sh'lah HaKadosh wrote that, in addition to the literal meaning of the words, the verse also alludes to the fire of anger and dispute. On the Sabbath, a person must be extra careful not to grow angry or to become involved in any dispute.

(Love Your Neighbor)

39

Baked Chicken with Honey Orange Sauce

1 3-4 lb. (1½-2 kg.) chicken,
  cut into pieces
2 eggs, beaten
2 cups bread crumbs
salt

pepper
1 cup orange juice
½-1 cup honey
½ cup water

Preheat oven to 350° F (175° C). Combine bread crumbs, salt and pepper. Roll chicken pieces in egg, then in bread crumbs and place in pan. Cover and bake for 15 minutes. Mix orange juice, honey and water. Pour over chicken. Bake for additional 30-45 minutes until tender. Serve hot or cold.

Southern Style Chicken with Yams

4 large yams
1 onion, sliced
salt
pepper
1 3-4 lb. (1½-2 kg.) chicken,
  cut into pieces

¼ cup walnuts
2 Tbsp. mustard
¼ cup honey
¼ cup orange juice

Preheat oven to 350° F (175° C). Peel yams, cut into big chunks and arrange in bottom of baking pan. Add sliced onion, salt and pepper. Place chicken in pan on top of yams. Mix remaining ingredients and pour over chicken. Cover with aluminum foil and bake until tender, about ¾-1 hour. Uncover and bake until brown. (If this must remain in oven for extended time Friday night, cover loosely with foil). Serve warm.

Whatever one does on Friday, be it preparing the food, the home or oneself, he should say "I am doing this in honor of the Holy Sabbath" out loud.

(Hida, *Avodat HaKodesh*)

How does one fulfill the requirement of *oneg* — Sabbath pleasure? Our Sages recommended preparing an especially rich dish and an aromatic beverage — more or less, in accordance with one's means. The more a man spends on the Sabbath and the more he prepares delectable foods — the more praiseworthy is he!

(Maimonides)

40

Chicken Cacciatore

1 onion
1 green pepper
1-2 Tbsp. oil
1 cup celery
2 tsp. oregano
¼ cup tomato purée

1 3-4 lb. (1½-2 kg.) chicken,
   cut into pieces
1 tsp. garlic powder
1 tsp. salt
hot cooked rice (optional)

Chop onion, green pepper and celery. Brown in oil in a large skillet. Add oregano and tomato purée. Rub chicken with salt and garlic. Add chicken to let it cook for about 1½ hours. Serve with rice if desired.

Chicken Loaf

2 lb (1 kg.) ground raw chicken
5 medium onions
2 eggs, beaten

1½ cups bread or challah crumbs
oil for frying

Grate 3 medium onions and combine with chicken, egg and bread crumbs. Mixture should be stiff. Add a bit more crumbs if necessary. Form into 3 loaves. Heat oil in large skillet and brown loaves on both sides till dark and crusty. Remove loaves from skillet and place on a platter. Slice 2 remaining onions and fry in remaining oil until golden. Place onions in a pot, add loaves and just enough water to cover them. Cover and cook for 1 hour. Add water if necessary. Can be served hot or cold.

Chicken Salad Supreme

½-¾ cup mayonnaise
2½ cups cooked diced chicken
1½ cups diced celery
¼ cup broken pecan meats

¼ cup sliced olives
½ tsp. salt
dash of freshly ground pepper
5 tomatoes or green peppers

Lightly toss together the chicken, celery, pecans, olives and seasonings. Add the mayonnaise, blending it in lightly. Serve in opened green pepper or cut a tomato in 5 wedges, press the sections apart and fill the tomato with chicken salad.

One should be careful to designate a special garment in honor of the Sabbath.

(Ben Ish Hai)

All the days of the week draw sustenance from the Sabbath; the Sabbath is the day on which the wheel of the six weekdays turns. It is a kind of root for the other days and will shed some of its sanctity on every day. That is why we refer to days of the week also as "Yemei Shabbatah". Some of the influence of the Sabbath is present in each and every weekday.

(Reshis Chochma)

41

Best Ever Roast Turkey

1 turkey up to 15 lbs. (7 kg.)	paprika
garlic powder	3-4 stalks celery

Preheat oven to 450° F (225° C). Wash turkey. Sprinkle with garlic powder and paprika. Put 3 or 4 stalks of celery in cavity. Wrap each leg in foil. Lay bird on its side and roast for 45 minutes. Turn to other side and roast a ½ hour longer.

Turn oven off and leave turkey in oven for 30 more minutes (or longer) before carving.

This method may be used for turkeys weighing up to 15 lbs. (7 kg.). No matter how you have made your turkeys in the past, you will be delighted with the juicy results you get with this method. Delicious hot or cold. Allow ¾ lb. (or 300 gm.) per person. *Note:* If you wish to stuff a turkey, do not use the above method. Instead, roast it slowly, in a 350° F (175° C) oven, allowing about 20 minutes per pound. Baste from time to time.

Veal Shoulder Roast

1 3 lb. (1½ kg.) veal shoulder roast	½ tsp. pepper
2 tsp. paprika	2 Tbsp. oil
1 tsp. garlic powder	canned mushrooms (optional)

Wash roast and put into a plastic cooking bag. Combine paprika, garlic powder, pepper and oil. Pour the mixture into the bag, close it with its fastener and shake the roast so that it gets coated with the mixture. Roast for 1½-2 hours, until fork tender at 350° F (175° C). Cool completely, then slice thinly and place into shallow pan. Pour gravy over it. Canned mushrooms may be added now. Before Shabbos, reheat on top of stove or in oven, covered. To serve cold in the morning, remove from gravy before refrigerating. Serves 8.

Variation: Instead of using a cooking bag, brush oil mixture onto surface of veal, wrap in foil and place in roasting pan. Baste while roasting.

It is incumbent on every man to be very, very zealous in making the Sabbath preparations; to be prompt and diligent like a man who has heard that the queen is coming to lodge at his house, or that the bride and her entourage are coming to his home. What would such a man do?

He would rejoice greatly and exclaim: "What a great honor they do me by their coming to dwell under my roof!"

He would say to his servants: "Arrange the house, clean and tidy it, and prepare the beds in honor of the guests, and I will go to purchase the bread, meat and fish — whatever I can obtain in their honor."

In such a case, a man would take upon himself the preparation of the

Beef Bourguignon

2 lb (1 kg.) stew beef   thyme
oil   parsley
2 Tbsp. flour   1 bay leaf
1 onion, sliced   salt
1 clove garlic, pressed   pepper
½ cup water   mushrooms (optional)
½ cup red wine

Brown meat in a little oil. Sprinkle with flour and add onions, garlic, water and wine. Add seasonings and mushrooms. Simmer covered for about 2½ hours. Serve hot. Serves 6.

Gedempte Fleish (Stewed Beef) with Apricots

8 oz. (200 gm.) dried apricots   1 bay leaf
4 cups water   1 Tbsp. lemon juice
2 onions, diced   2 Tbsp. brown sugar
4 lb. (2 kg.) beef shoulder   1 tsp. cinnamon
2 Tbsp. oil

Wash and soak apricots for 1 hour. Brown onions and meat in fat. Add remaining ingredients plus apricots and water. Cover and cook over low heat 2½ hours or until meat is tender.

food, even if he had a thousand servants.

Now, who is greater than the Sabbath, which is both bride and queen and is called delightful? Surely, the master of the house should himself be involved in Sabbath preparations, though he may have countless servants.

(Sefer Chasidim)

Always slice across the grain when carving meat to prevent a stringy texture. Roast beef cuts more easily if allowed to cool for 30 minutes.

Pot Roast

4 lb. (2 kg.) brisket
1 stalk celery
1 onion
3 cloves garlic
oil
3 carrots

½ cup red wine (optional)
½ cup chopped tomato
½ cup water
1 bay leaf
salt
pepper

Dice celery, onion and garlic cloves. Sauté in oil until soft. Add meat and brown. Add remaining ingredients. Cover and simmer 2½ to 3 hours until tender. Cool and slice. (Meat slices easily when cold). To serve Friday night, replace sliced beef in gravy and keep warm. Sliced beef is also delicious cold. Serves 12.

Tongue peels easily while hot, or very warm.

Tongue Polonaise

1 medium tongue, pickled or plain
¼ cup brown sugar
1 cup puréed apricots
2 Tbsp. ketchup

2 tsp. lemon juice
½ cup raisins
orange juice

Boil tongue in water to cover about 2 hours or until tender. Peel and slice while still warm. Combine remaining ingredients in saucepan, adding as much orange juice as needed for sauce-like consistency. Add sliced tongue, cover and cook for 10-15 minutes to absorb flavor. Serve hot. Serves 6-8, depending on size of tongue.

Corned Beef Piquant

1 corned beef brisket
1 onion, sliced
3-4 cloves garlic

10-12 whole cloves
½ cup maple syrup

Each man's income for the entire year is determined between Rosh Hashanah and Yom Kippur — with the exception of Sabbath and festival expenses and the cost of Torah education for his children. These are granted in accordance with the man's outlay. If he spends little for these, he will be given little; if he spends more, he will be given more.

(Talmud Bavli)

Place pickled beef in pot. Cover with water. Add onion and garlic. Boil covered for about 2½ hours or more until tender. Remove beef from pot and transfer to roasting pan. Stud beef all over with cloves. Pour maple syrup over meat. Bake 30 minutes in 350° F (175° C) oven, basting several times. For even better results, put clove-studded beef in a plastic roasting bag. Allow ½ lb. (or ¼ kg.) meat for each adult (generous serving).

Meat Loaf

Combine in a large bowl:

2 lbs. (1 kg.) ground beef or veal
1 cup soft bread crumbs
¼ cup wheat germ (optional)
2 Tbsp. minced onion

½ tsp. garlic powder
¾ cup tomato juice or chicken soup
2 eggs, slightly beaten
oil

Mix all ingredients well and pack into a loaf pan. Sprinkle a little oil on top. Bake at 350° F (175° C) until done (about 40 minutes). Serves 6-8.
Variations: 1) Cover loaf with ketchup or a seasoned tomato sauce before baking. 2) Pack half the mixture into the pan. Arrange 3 or 4 whole peeled hard-boiled eggs in a row down the center and then cover with remaining mixture. Slice and serve cold at the morning meal.

It is impossible to forget the Sabbath; its very mention brings to mind a sweet fragance. On the Sabbath, the dove found a resting place and so, too, will the tired and weary find tranquility and peace therein.

(Zemiroth)

Swedish Meatballs

2 lbs. (1 kg.) ground beef
1 potato
1 onion

1½ cups ketchup
1½ cups water
2 heaping Tbsp. brown sugar

Grate potato and onion into ground beef. Form into balls. Mix together ketchup, water and brown sugar. Bring to a boil and add meat balls. Simmer ¾-1 hour. (Leftover sauce can be frozen and reused). Serve hot with rice or mashed potatoes. Serves 8.

Rabbi Isaac Luria was careful to eat his Sabbath repast on a table with four legs similar to the table in the Holy Temple.

(*Aruch Ha-shulchan*)

ACCOMPANIMENTS

Onion Challah Stuffing

2 cups chopped onions
4 cups water with 1 Tbsp. salt
3 cups dry challah crumbs
½-1 cup chopped tart apples (optional)
1 egg

½ cup oil
1 tsp. salt
¼ tsp. paprika
1 Tbsp. poultry seasoning

A bird should be stuffed just before it is ready to roast. The combination of poultry and stuffing ingredients is tempting to dangerous bacteria if left for any length of time.

Boil water and salt. Add onions and simmer 10 minutes. Drain. Add remaining ingredients and mix well. Moisten with chicken soup. Stuff chicken and bake. Extra stuffing can be roasted alongside chicken in roasting pan.

Challah Stuffing

1 large challah
6 eggs
2 large onions, diced and fried

1 cup sugar
cinnamon
3 Tbsp. onion soup mix

Fresh lemon juice removes onion and fish scent from hands.

Soak challah in water and squeeze well. Pull apart into tiny pieces. Mix with remaining ingredients. Stuff into roasting chicken.
Variation: Heat oil to cover bottom of baking pan till very hot. Pour in stuffing. Bake 1 hour at 350° F (175° C).

46

Helzel (Stuffed Fowl Neck)

2 Tbsp. matzah meal, semolina
  or bread crumbs
2 Tbsp. flour
6 Tbsp. chopped onion
salt

pepper
¼ cup chicken fat or margarine
½ tsp. chicken soup powder
1 helzel (skin from fowl neck)

Mix first 7 ingredients together. Loosely fill the neck skin and sew up ends. Roast helzel under chicken, turkey, goose or duck for same length of time as the poultry. Baste occasionally.

Cholents

Known by many different names in the world's Jewish communities, it is nonetheless the dish which is universally unique to the Sabbath.

Since cooking is prohibited on the Sabbath but hot food is appropriate, some dish had to be devised which could be left to simmer on a covered fire or hotplate, untouched from before sunset on Friday until the following day.

It became a matter of principle to serve hot food on the Sabbath morning in the time of the Saduccees some 2000 years ago. Seeking to differ with the G-d-given interpretation of the Torah in our Oral tradition, they redefined the verse: "You shall kindle no fire ... on the Sabbath day" to mean that no fires might burn at all (even if kindled before the Sabbath). While the Sadducees sat in darkness, partaking of cold foods, loyal Jews filled their homes with light each Sabbath eve and prepared dishes to be kept warm so that the Sabbath might be enjoyed in the manner intended by the Creator.

Beef Cholent

3 Tbsp. oil
2 Tbsp. sugar
6-7 potatoes
½ cup barley
½ cup lima beans
½ cup kidney beans (optional)
meat bones

1 onion
1 or 2 lbs. (½ to 1 kg.) meat
   (chuck or flanken)
2-3 tsp. salt
½ tsp. pepper
Gravy from roasted chicken or
   meat for added flavor (optional)

In large pot brown the sugar in oil. Immediately add 1 cup water. Peel and cut potatoes into chunks and add to water. Check beans and barley carefully for insects, rinse and add to pot. Add remaining ingredients. Add water just to cover mixture. Bring to a boil. Cook covered on a low flame for 1-2 hours. Add water to cover and bring to boil. Place on covered fire (*blech*) before Shabbos and keep close to flame overnight but not directly over it. It should simmer gently. Serves 6-10.

Variation: Substitute 1 chicken for meat.

Prune Cholent

2 lbs. (1 kg.) meat
½ cup margarine, oil or other fat
2 onions sliced
2 lbs. (1 kg.) potatoes

¼ cup honey
1 lb. (500 gm.) prunes
1 tsp. salt
1 cup water

Brown meat in fat, add onions and stir until brown. Pit prunes and add with other ingredients. Bring to a boil. Cook 1 hour before placing on a covered fire (*blech*). Serves 8-12.

Chicken Cholent

3 onions	½ cup lima beans
oil	½ cup barley
1 chicken, cut in serving pieces	water
5 potatoes	

Slice onions. Fry in a little oil until golden brown. Add pieces of chicken and cook until the skin browns (about 10 minutes). Add potatoes, peeled or unpeeled, cut in large pieces. Add beans and barley. Add water to cover, plus 1 additional cup and cook for at least 1 hour. Before putting the cholent on a covered fire (*blech*) add another cup of water. Cover cholent and keep it on a low-medium covered flame. *Variation:* For extra Shabbos flavor, add kneidlach and some additional water after you have cooked the cholent for a ½-hour.

To insure a lovely brown color, add 1 Tbsp. honey, or carmelize 2 Tbsp. sugar when browning onions.

Vegetarian Cholent

1 large onion, sliced or diced	5 Tbsp. onion soup powder
2 Tbsp. oil	4 carrots, cut in chunks
1 cup barley, soaked for several hours	4 medium potatoes, cut in chunks
1 cup split peas, soaked for several hours	water

Sauté onion in oil in pot until soft, then add rest of ingredients with water to cover. Bring to a boil and cook for at least 1 hour, adding water as needed to keep a soupy consistency. Place cholent on covered fire (*blech*).
Variations:
1. Add kishke and simmer for 20 minutes before putting on covered fire.
2. Chunks of meat substitute may be added for extra texture and to make it more interesting.
3. Well-washed raw eggs may be carefully immersed in the cholent before putting it on the covered flame. At serving time, remove eggs, and peel. They turn brown. Serve them separately.

So-called "traditional Jewish" foods are most often not Jewish at all, but recipes borrowed and adapted from the host culture in countries where we sojourned.

The three foods which are uniquely Jewish in that they are in direct response to our halachah are matzah, cholent or hamin, and gefilte fish.

Cholent with Whole Wheat Kishke

1 cup red kidney beans
1 cup baby lima beans
½ cup barley
4-5 potatoes
1 sweet potato (optional)

2-3 onions
1-2 Tbsp. oil (optional)
2 Tbsp. ketchup
2 Tbsp. brown sugar
garlic powder to taste

Soak beans and check for insects. Slice onions and place on bottom of large sauce pan with oil, if desired. Add beans, potatoes and barley. Cover with water. Boil 10 minutes. Add ketchup, brown sugar and garlic powder. Boil 20 minutes longer. Place baked whole wheat *kishke* on top of cholent while still wrapped in foil. Put pot on covered fire (*blech*) overnight.

Whole Wheat Kishke

2 stalks celery
1 carrot, shredded
1 large onion, shredded
½ cup oil

1½ cups whole wheat flour
2 tsp. paprika
garlic powder, herbs (optional)

Blend all ingredients except flour and paprika until coarsely chopped in blender. Mix in flour and paprika. Divide batter into half. Wrap each half in aluminum foil to form loaf. Fasten ends and top securely. Bake on a baking sheet at 350° F (175° C) for 45 minutes. Turn loaves over and bake about 45 minutes longer. Place in cholent in aluminum foil. Remove foil to slice and serve.
Variation: After baking 1½ hours, open foil a bit for additional browning and bake 10-15 minutes longer.

"It was said of Shammai the Elder: Every day he ate in honor of the Sabbath. If he chanced upon a fine animal, he would set it aside for the Sabbath. When he found one finer than the first, he would set the second aside, eating the first."

(Talmud Bavli)

When inviting guests for Shabbos, ask them in advance if they have any special diet requirements. This can spare embarrassment and discomfort, and – most of all – enable you to fulfill the mitzvah of hachnosas orchim (welcoming guests) properly.

Parve Cholent

2 cups lima beans (medium sized)	5 carrots
1 cup barley	5 potatoes
4 onions	2 bay leaves (optional)
5 cloves garlic	salt, pepper to taste
2-3 tsp. margarine	2 tsp. honey (optional)
4-5 stalks celery	

Check beans and barley. Sauté onions and garlic in margarine. Cut celery and carrots. Slice potatoes in halves. Place vegetables in large pot. Fill to three-quarters with water. Add bay leaves, salt, pepper and honey and bring to a boil. Cook 1-1½ hours before placing on covered heat (*blech*).

Checking beans for insects is easy if you bring them to a boil with 3 cups water for each cup of beans. Let cool for 2 hrs in pot. This allows the beans to absorb water and expand and their skins become transparent. Drain rinse and check.

Moroccan Hamin

Flanken
chick peas (1 can)
wheat grains (1 pkg)
pearl onions (10)
olive oil (3 TBS.)

1 chicken, cut in serving pieces or 2 lbs. (1 kg.) meat	2 tsp. turmeric
	salt
3 potatoes	pepper
1 cup fresh or frozen peas	1 medium onion
1 tsp. cumin	2 tsp. garlic powder
paprika	6 hard boiled eggs with shells

Cube potatoes. Sprinkle chicken with paprika. Put everything except peas into the pot. Add water until pot is ½ full. Cover, bring to a boil. Turn down flame to its lowest level and simmer 45 minutes. Add peas on top of hamin. Do not mix. Sprinkle with paprika, simmer an additional 10 minutes. Put on covered flame before Shabbat.

Check the level of water right before Shabbos to make sure the cholent won't be too dry.

Israeli Hamin

3 cups rice (checked)
1 large tomato, peeled and grated
   or ¼ cup tomato paste
1-2 carrots, shredded
1 large apple, peeled and shredded
1 Tbsp. salt
1 tsp. pepper
1 tsp. cinnamon

2 large onions, diced
½ cup oil
4 large potatoes, cut in
   thick slices
1 chicken, cut in serving pieces
parsley
3-4 cloves garlic

Mix together rice, tomato, carrots, apple, salt, pepper and cinnamon. Using a large pot, brown onion in oil. Arrange potatoes on top of browned onions. Spread rice mixture over potatoes. Arrange chicken pieces on top of rice mixture. Add parsley and garlic. Add water to cover plus 2 cups. Bring to boil and simmer for one hour before placing on covered flame or hot plate.
Variation: Coat chicken pieces with tomato paste for extra flavor and color.

Make sure the cholent is kept barely simmering until it is served. If it is merely kept warm it will sour.

Halim (Persian Hamin)

1 whole chicken
1 cup rice
1 onion diced
¼ tsp. + ½ tsp. turmeric
½ tsp. + 1 tsp. cumin

½ tsp. + 1 tsp. salt
¼ tsp. + ¼ tsp. pepper
1½ cups whole wheat grains
2 cups diced leek (optional)

Check rice and rinse. Combine rice with diced onion, ¼ tsp. turmeric, ½ tsp. salt, ½ tsp. cumin, ¼ tsp. pepper. Remove fat from chicken, dice, and add to rice. Cook rice in 1½ cups water. Stuff chicken with rice mixture and tie thread around chicken to hold together. (Or put the rice mixture into a cloth). Check wheat and rinse. Boil wheat in 3 cups boiling water, adding ½ tsp. turmeric, 1 tsp. salt, 1 tsp. cumin, ½ tsp. pepper. Add stuffed chicken and leek. Cook for ½-1 hour. Adjust seasonings and water before placing on covered flame before Shabbat.

Line the cholent pot with waxed paper or a margarine wrapper to make cleaning easier.

ACCOMPANIMENTS:

Delicious Cholent Kishke

1½ cups flour
½ cup margarine
½ tsp. pepper
½ tsp. potato flour

4 Tbsp. onion, chopped
1 tsp. salt
1½ tsp. paprika

Combine ingredients. Wrap in foil or a piece of cloth. Before Shabbos, place in boiling cholent or soup for at least 1 hour.

Vegetable Kishke

2 stalks celery, or 1 medium zucchini
1 large onion
3 carrots
1 small potato
1½ tsp. salt

⅛ tsp. pepper
1 tsp. paprika
3 cups sifted flour
¾ cup oil

Shred vegetables. Add remaining ingredients and mix well. Form into a loaf, wrap in aluminum foil. Roast with chicken or place directly into boiling cholent for at least 1 hour before Shabbos. Freezes well raw. A few loaves may be prepared in advance and frozen in aluminum foil.

And it came to pass that on the sixth day they gathered twice as much bread (lechem mishneh) two omers for each person and all the rulers of the congregation came and told Moses. And he said to them, "This is what the L-rd said, 'Tomorrow is the rest of the holy Sabbath of the L-rd. Bake that which you will bake [today], cook that which you will cook [today], and that which remains leave over until the morning.'" And they left it over until the morning, as Moses commanded, and it did not stink nor was there any worm in it. And Moses said, "Eat it today for today is the Sabbath of the L-rd. Today you shall not find it in the field. Six days shall you gather it but the seventh day is the Sabbath — there shall be none."

(Exodus 16)

Wonderful Cholent Kneidl

⅔ cup self-rising flour
3 Tbsp. solet (semolina farina)
½ tsp. salt
pepper

1 beaten egg
4 Tbsp. water
½ cup. (100 gm.) margarine
dash nutmeg (optional)

Cut margarine into chunks. Mix remaining ingredients and combine carefully with margarine so that the chunks remain in large pieces. Form large ball. Place in boiling cholent 20 minutes before Shabbos. It doesn't keep its shape, but it's delicious! Serves 4.

Kugels

No side dish identifies the Sabbath meal like a kugel.

Many cooks prepare one kugel in honor of the Sabbath. Some families serve extra kugels in honor of a *Yom Tov* or *Rosh Chodesh* that falls on a Sabbath. Their idea is to serve as many kugels as there are Torah scrolls read in the synagogue.

Kugel recipes run the gamut from sweet to salty, soft to crisp, bland to sharp. They may be baked in the oven or pan-fried on the range. Served hot or cold, a kugel makes any *Kiddush* something special.

Kugel defies definition or translation — it simply must be tasted.

Lokshen Kugel

8 oz. (250 gm.) wide noodles	1 tsp. cinnamon
3 eggs	½ cup raisins
2 Tbsp. margarine	juice of 1 lemon
1 cup sugar	

Preheat oven to 350° F (175° C). Boil and drain noodles. Melt margarine in frying pan and add cooked noodles, stirring until all margarine is absorbed. Separate eggs. Beat yolks. Add yolks, sugar, cinnamon and raisins and lemon juice to noodles. Mix well. Beat egg whites until stiff. Fold them into noodle mixture. Pour into a small, well-greased casserole dish. Bake for 30-40 minutes. Serves 6.

Salt and Pepper Lokshen Kugel

8 oz. (250 gm.) thin noodles	½ tsp. salt
2-3 eggs	½ tsp. pepper
1 Tbsp. oil	oil for pan

Cook noodles in salted water. Drain. When slightly cooled, stir in remaining ingredients. To bake: pour into well-greased pan. Bake in oven for 45 minutes at 350° F (175° C) until brown. To fry: Generously grease and heat a large frying pan. Pour in noodle mixture. Turn down heat to very low. Cover and cook for 30 to 40 minutes. Cool entirely. Turn over and cook on the other side uncovered for 10-15 minutes, on lowest heat until brown. Best served hot or rewarmed over another pot.

Variation: Use whole wheat noodles.

Old Fashioned Yerushalmi Kugel

1 lb. (400 gm.) thin noodles	4 eggs
1 cup sugar	1½ tsp. salt
¾ cup oil	2 tsp. black pepper

Cook noodles according to package instructions. Drain and set aside. Caramelize sugar in oil over low to medium flame until deep golden brown. Watch carefully to prevent burning. Pour noodles into caramelized sugar and stir, coating all noodles with the syrup. Keeping the fire very low, stir in eggs, salt and pepper to taste and more sugar, if desired. Mix entire contents and cook on low flame for 10-15 minutes. To bake: Pour into a well-greased pan and bake in a medium oven for ¾-1 hour, till crispy and dark on top. To fry: Heat 2-3 Tbsp. oil in a medium-large pot. When oil is hot, pour in noodle mixture. Cover and cook over a medium-high flame for 5 minutes, until kugel is set. Continue cooking ½-hour over low heat. Cool *entirely*. Remove onto a large plate. Invert and cook other side similarly. Remove from heat before serving. Allow to cool slightly before inverting pot to remove kugel. Serve with sliced pickle. Serves 10-12.
Variation: Outside Jerusalem, a similar, but sweeter kugel is made. Omit pepper, decrease salt to 1 tsp. and add ½ cup raisins. Though this kugel lacks the taste of Jerusalem, it still is delicious.

If you want to keep this kugel on the covered fire overnight, add 1 cup water before Shabbos and leave on a hot part of the blech.

Shortcut Yerushalmi Kugel

1 lb. (400 gm.) thin noodles	4 eggs
1 quart (1 liter) boiling water	1½ Tbsp. salt
1 cup sugar	2 tsp. black pepper
½ cup oil	

Pour boiling water over noodles and let stand in pot until thoroughly absorbed. Meanwhile, melt ¾ cup sugar over a low fire until dark brown. Add oil and continue simmering for 3 minutes. Pour sugar and oil over noodles. Add rest of ingredients and mix well. Bake in well-greased pan in medium oven 350° F (175° C) for one hour or cook on top of fire for 1 hour on a low flame. Grease the pot well. Don't fill pot more than 4 inches (10 cm.) high or kugel will not cook through. Serves about 10.

Rabbi Chisda said: One should always awake early on Friday to prepare for the Sabbath as it says "and they shall prepare what they shall bring" (Exodus 16).

(Talmud Bavli)

Apple Noodle Kugel

1 lb. (400 gm.) thin noodles
1 cup oil
1 cup sugar
2 tsp. cinnamon

3 large apples
1 cup raisins
3 eggs

Cook and drain noodles. Peel and dice apples. Mix all ingredients thoroughly. Pour into large greased casserole dish. Bake for 45 minutes at 350° F (175° C). Serves 10.

Fruit Noodle Kugel

8 oz. (250 gm.) wide egg noodles
3-4 eggs
½ cup sugar
1 tsp. cinnamon
½ tsp. salt

1½ cups canned fruit pieces,
    well drained
½ cup margarine
½ cup brown sugar
1 cup (or more) cornflakes

Boil noodles in a large pot. Drain and rinse with cold water. Add beaten eggs, sugar, cinnamon, salt and fruit. Place in medium-sized, greased casserole dish. Melt margarine. Crush cornflakes slightly. Mix margarine and brown sugar. Add cornflakes to make a crumbly topping, and sprinkle evenly over kugel. Bake for 1¼-1½ hours at 350° F (175° C).

When the L-rd announced that He was giving the Torah to the people of Israel, He said: "If you fulfill all these commandments, you will inherit the World to Come!"

The people asked: "Master of the Universe, won't you show us a sample of that World in this world?"

And so He replied: "Here is the Sabbath. It will bring you a small taste of the pleasure and peace of the World to Come."

(*Osios D'Rabbi Akiva*)

Quick Pineapple Kugel

8 oz. (250 gm.) fine or medium
    egg noodles
½ cup margarine
¾ cup sugar

3 eggs
½ tsp. vanilla
½ can pineapple slices

Cook noodles and drain. Place remaining ingredients in a blender. Blend until smooth. Combine this purée with the noodles. Bake in a greased 9- by 13-inch pan or in a greased 2½ quart casserole, at 375° F (190° C) for 1 hour. Serves 8.

To avoid water boiling over when cooking noodles, grease top inch of pot.

Kasha Noodle Kugel

1 cup kasha (buckwheat groats)	2 cups cooked noodles
4 eggs	1½ tsp. salt
2 medium onions, chopped	½ tsp. pepper
¼ cup oil	½ tsp. garlic powder
2 cups boiling water	3 Tbsp. oil for pan

Check kasha. Beat 1 egg and mix with kasha until all kasha is coated. Meanwhile, sauté onion in oil until it starts to brown. Pour in kasha, and add 2 cups boiling water. Stir, cover pot and lower heat to simmer for 15 minutes. Water should then be absorbed and kasha ready. Combine kasha with noodles. Add seasonings, and then 3 beaten eggs. Pour 3 Tbsp. oil into 2½-quart (2½ liter) casserole. Pour in kasha-noodle mixture. Bake in a 350° F (175° C) oven about 40 minutes.

In Poland it was customary to eat kasha with gravy on the Sabbath. The Kadosh of Strelisk attributed this custom to a play on the word "kasha." By eating kasha we express the wish that all our questions — "kashas" in Yiddish — be resolved!
(Ohr HaShabbos)

Potato Kugel

3-4 medium potatoes	¼ cup flour or matzah meal
1 onion	2-2½ tsp. salt
2 eggs	1 tsp. pepper
⅓ cup oil	

Preheat oven to 375° F (190° C). Grate or grind potatoes and onion. Combine with other ingredients. Pour into greased baking dish and bake for 1-1½ hours until golden brown and knife inserted in middle comes out clean. If there is a delay in baking, sprinkle matzah meal (or flour) over the grated potatoes to prevent discoloration. Stir in just before baking. Serves about 8.

Mashed Potato Kugel

3 medium potatoes	salt
1 onion	pepper
3 eggs	oil

If you're boiling potatoes anyway, add a few more and make a mashed potato kugel.

Boil potatoes and mash while hot. Sauté chopped onion in oil until translucent. Mix potatoes, fried onion and eggs together. Season with salt and pepper to taste. Place mixture in oiled baking dish. Spread top with a little oil. Bake in 350° F (175° C) oven until top is golden brown.

Zucchini Kugel

2-3 lbs. (1-1½ kg.) zucchini (approximately 12 medium)	3 Tbsp. bran
1 cup sliced onion	¾ cup bread crumbs
2 cloves garlic, minced	2 eggs
2 Tbsp. oil	1 tsp. salt
2 Tbsp. margarine	½ tsp. pepper
	½ tsp. curry powder

Peel and slice the squash. Sauté, along with the onions and garlic in margarine and oil until mixture browns and becomes partially crisp. Add a tablespoon of water, stir and cover mixture for a few minutes, cooking until water is absorbed. Add bran, breadcrumbs, eggs and seasonings. Pour into greased loaf pan, or round kugel pan. Bake for 45 minutes at 350° F (175° C). Serves 8-10.

Carrot Kugel

2 cups grated carrots	1 tsp. baking powder
3 Tbsp. lemon or orange juice	½ tsp. baking soda
1 cup margarine	1 tsp. salt
½ cup brown sugar	½ tsp. cinnamon
1 egg	½ cup raisins
1½ cups flour	

Preheat oven to 350° F (175° C). Grate carrots and add juice to prevent discoloration. Mix margarine, sugar and egg. Add dry ingredients, raisins and finally carrots, mixing well. Bake in greased pan for 1 hour. Serves 8.

Whole Wheat Carrot Kugel

1 cup oil	1 cup wheat germ
½ cup honey	1 tsp. baking soda
4 eggs	1 tsp. baking powder
2 Tbsp. lemon juice	½ tsp. salt
1½ cups whole wheat flour	3 cups grated carrots

Preheat oven to 350° F (175° C). Combine oil, honey, eggs and lemon juice. Mix well. Add dry ingredients. Stir in carrots. Bake in large greased pan for 45-60 minutes. Serves 8.

Sabbath candles bring peace to heaven and earth and drive out evil from our homes.
(*Sidduro shel Shabbos*)

If one is blessed and able to provide abundant food and delicacies, he should invite the poor and needy to partake of his repast... What a great pleasure it is to help others and see them happy through the food and kind words one has given.
(*Siddur Bais Yaakov*)

Sweet Potato Kugel

1 large sweet potato	⅓ cup oil
1 potato	¾ cup sugar
1 carrot	pinch of salt
2 apples	1 tsp. cinnamon
rind and juice of ½ lemon	½ cup raisins (optional)
⅓ cup matzah meal	

Shred vegetables and apples. Combine all ingredients, mixing well. Spread in greased casserole. Bake covered at 325° F (165° C) for 45 minutes. Uncover and bake an additional 15 minutes.

There are seven gates to the soul — two eyes, two ears, two nostrils, and a mouth.

The Creator blessed the seventh day of the week and sanctified it. It is therefore fitting that the mouth — which is the seventh gateway — give praise, through song, prayer and Torah learning all through the day.

(Rabbi Moshe Azulai)

Kraut Kugel

5 cups finely shredded cabbage	⅓ cup potato flour
2 tsp. salt	¾ cup sliced blanched almonds
⅓ cup fat	¼ cup seedless white raisins
½ cup boiling water	2 Tbsp. sugar
1½ cups cubed white bread or challah	4 eggs

Cook the cabbage and salt in fat over low flame for 30 minutes, stirring frequently. Cool. Pour water over bread and squeeze dry. Mash. Add the potato flour, raisins, almonds and sugar. Separate the eggs and stir yolks into mixture. Add cabbage and mix until thoroughly combined. Beat the egg whites until stiff but not dry, and fold into the mixture. Turn into a greased 2 quart (2 liter) casserole dish. Bake at 350° F (175° C) for 40 minutes or until set. Serves 8.

You shall lack nothing on the Sabbath. Eat, be satisfied and bless your G-d whom you love, because He has blessed you beyond all nations.

(Zemiroth)

62

Barley Kugel

1 cup pearl barley
4 cups water
2 tsp. salt
8 oz. (200 gm.) chopped mushrooms

2 onions, sliced
2 Tbsp. margarine
¼ tsp. pepper
2 eggs, beaten

Check barley for insects and rinse. Boil water and stir in barley. Bring back to a boil. Add salt, cover and cook over low heat about 1 hour or until soft. Drain. Brown the mushrooms and onions in the margarine. Add to the barley with pepper and eggs. Taste for seasoning. Turn into a greased baking dish or casserole. Bake in a 350° F (175° C) oven for 40 minutes or until brown and set. Serves 6.

Challah Kugel

1 small challah or 8 slices of bread
4 eggs
1 cup sugar

2 tsp. cinnamon
1 cup diced fruit (e.g. apples, pears,
    peaches, raisins or canned fruit)

Pour hot water over challah. Squeeze out the water and tear challah into shreds. Stir in eggs, sugar, cinnamon and diced fruit (either 1 fruit or a combination). Mix well and bake in heavily greased pan for 45 minutes at 400° F (200° C) until brown. For a crusty bottom, heat a little oil in baking pan before pouring in mixture. Serves 8.

Friday night serving suggestion: Top challah kugel with following orange sauce.

Orange Sauce

4 tsp. cornstarch
4 tsp. sugar
pinch salt
10 Tbsp. water

10 Tbsp. orange juice
1 tsp. lemon juice
1 Tbsp. margarine

In small saucepan, combine first three ingredients. Add a small amount of the liquid and stir till dry ingredients are thoroughly combined. Add remaining ingredients and stir while bringing to a boil. Remove from heat. Keep warm on covered flame (*blech*) until kugel is served and serve in a gravy boat.

Walking in Jerusalem on a Friday, you will hear friends wishing one another "*a good Erev Shabbos*." The custom is explained this way: with two days' work to do in one, and the awareness of time passing by, we are especially susceptible on Friday to irritability and short temper. We therefore wish one another success in overcoming this pitfall and accomplishing the day's work with joy.

Rice Kugel

1½ cups raw rice   ½ cup raisins
6 eggs   ⅓ cup oil
½ cup brown sugar

Preheat oven to 350° F (175° C). Check rice and cook according to directions on package. Remove from heat, drain, and add remaining ingredients. Bake in 2 quart (2 liter) ungreased dish for 1 hour. Serves 8.

This story was told by the Rebbe, Rav Nechemia Alter. Once I went for Shabbos to the home of the famous tzaddik, Rav Pinatchi, of Piltz. I arrived Thursday towards evening. After supper, we discussed Torah issues at length and the tzaddik was in a state of great joy. When I retired to my room, I heard a strange chanting from the room next to mine. Listening carefully I recognized the voice of my host, who seemed to be pacing, and speaking in a soft, prayerful voice: "Master of the Universe, may it be Thy Will that the kugel for Shabbos Kodesh turn out especially delicious in honor of my guest. And when Shabbos begins, may the sanctity of the day enter my body, my home, and all the dishes prepared specially for Shabbos." To my surprise he continued to chant thus for a long, long time....

(*Sippurei Chasidim*, Zevin)

Delicious Rolled Apple Kugel

1 cup brown sugar   2 tsp. baking powder
1 cup hot water   ½ tsp. salt
3 apples   4 Tbsp. oil
½ tsp. cinnamon   ½ cup water or juice (scant)
1½ cup flour

Mix hot water and brown sugar in small, greased rectangular baking pan. Peel and thinly slice apples, into a bowl. Sprinkle with cinnamon. Set inside. In another bowl, mix dry ingredients, oil and water to form a soft dough. Roll into a rectangle on a lightly floured surface. Spread apples over dough. Roll up like a jelly roll and slice in 1-inch (2.5 cm.) pieces. Place pieces side by side in pan with brown sugar mixture. Baste. Bake at 425° F (200° C) for 20 minutes.
Variation: This can be made in individual servings in a muffin tin. Place 1-2 Tbsp. of brown sugar sauce in each section and place rolled apple kugel pieces in each section. Bake 15 minutes. Serve warm or cold. Freezes well.

Kubana (Yemenite Kugel)

4 cups flour
7 Tbsp. margarine
½ oz. (10 gms.) yeast, dissolved
  in ¼ cup warm water

2 cups water, room temperature
½ tsp. salt, to taste
2 Tbsp. sugar, to taste

Mix together all ingredients, except for 4 Tbsp. margarine, and knead. Melt the 4 Tbsp. margarine in a kubana pot, or any pot made of thin metal with a tightly fitting lid. Place prepared dough loosely on top of melted margarine. Allow dough to rise in warm place to approximately double the size. Place lid tightly on pot. Put into 350° F (175° C) oven. Bake for approximately ½ hour. Cool. Turn kubana over to other side and bake for another ½ hour. Serve warm on Shabbat morning by placing on top of another pot on *blech*. This Yemenite specialty is usually served dipped in spicy sauces. It can also be enjoyed with salted tomato slices and hard-boiled eggs.
Variation: Increase sugar to 4-6 Tbsp. and sprinkle 4 Tbsp. sesame seeds over melted margarine. Place dough over sesame seeds. Turn over before baking. This version tastes like a cake, rather than a kugel.

Sanctify the Sabbath by choice meals, by beautiful garments, delight your soul with pleasure, and I will reward you for this very pleasure!

(D'vorim Rabbah)

Vegetables and Other Side Dishes

Vegetables and other produce need little preparation to add fine flavor to weekday meals. But the homemaker wants everything served on the Sabbath to be exceptional. Even a special ripple-edged knife for slicing the carrots or potatoes makes Sabbath vegetables a cut above the ordinary.

Since Sabbath foods are prepared in advance anyway, the cook takes extra time and care to dress everyday vegetables in their holiday best, transforming them into the royal side dishes fit for a Sabbath feast.

Honeyed Carrots

1 lb. (500 gm.) carrots
2 Tbsp. oil
½ tsp. salt

3 Tbsp. honey
juice of 2 oranges
handful of raisins

Slice carrots thinly. Pour the oil in bottom of a medium-sized saucepan. Put carrots in first, then the other ingredients. Cover and simmer about 1½ hours on a small flame, being careful not to let it burn. Serve hot. Serves 6.

Sweet Potato Tzimmes

4 sweet potatoes
6 carrots
¼ cup brown sugar
2 Tbsp. honey
¾ tsp. salt

1 Tbsp. margarine
½ tsp. ginger
½ tsp. cinnamon
1 cup water

Peel and dice sweet potatoes and carrots. Combine all ingredients in a saucepan. Cover and cook 1-2 hours over low heat. Serve hot. Serves 12.

Zucchini in Tomato Sauce

oil
1 large onion
1 green pepper
1 celery stalk

2 lbs. (1 kg.) zucchini, sliced
1 tsp. salt
1 cup tomato sauce
½ cup water

Sauté the onion, pepper and celery in a small amount of oil in a large pot. Add sliced zucchini. Add salt, water and tomato sauce. Cover and steam for 1 hour. Add a little more water if necessary. Serves 6-8.

Dilled Zucchini

8 medium zucchini squash
water
pinch sugar
1 tsp. salt

¼ tsp. pepper
1 Tbsp. margarine
1 Tbsp. snipped fresh dill stems

Wash squash well. Without peeling, slice diagonally into a saucepan. Cover with water. Add sugar, salt and pepper. Bring to a boil. Drain. Add margarine and dill. Toss. Refrigerate until just before Shabbos. Cover and reheat. Place on covered flame (*blech*) to keep hot, but not brown. Serves 6.

Easy Sunny Zucchini Bake

2 lbs. (1 kg.) zucchini
½ cup oil
4 eggs
1 cup flour
1 tsp. baking powder

1 onion, cut up
salt, pepper, sugar to taste
sweet paprika
parsley

Peel zucchini. Cut into cubes and set aside. Mix all other ingredients and combine with the zucchini. Place in a greased baking pan. Sprinkle top with sweet paprika and parsley. Bake at 350° F (175° C) for 30 minutes. Serve hot. Serves 6-8.

On every day of the week, we should eagerly anticipate the Sabbath. Imagine a man confined in prison for six days. On every day of his imprisonment he thinks of the day he is to be set free. He takes comfort in looking forward to that day on which he will be relieved from distress. The hoped-for day is cherished and eagerly awaited throughout.

(*Sha'arei Tefillah*)

When buying carrots, beets or squash, choose small or medium unblemished ones, which are sweeter and tastier than large ones.

Sautéed Mushrooms

1 lb. (500 gm.) mushrooms
2 Tbsp. oil
¼ tsp. salt

2 Tbsp. chopped onion
½ cup water

Wash mushrooms and drain. Slice or leave whole. Sauté onions until golden in oil. Add mushrooms and sauté additional 2-3 minutes. Season. Add water and cook covered for 10 minutes. Serves 4-8.

Sweet and Sour Beans

1½ lb. (750 gm.) fresh string beans
1 tsp. salt
⅛ tsp. pepper
1 bay leaf
3 cloves

2 Tbsp. sugar
4 Tbsp. vinegar
3 Tbsp. oil
water

Cut string beans into 1-inch pieces. Cover and steam in a little water. Add salt, pepper, bay leaf, cloves, sugar, vinegar and oil and cook for 5 minutes, stirring frequently until string beans are tender. Add a little water if necessary. Remove bay leaf. Serve hot or cold.
Serves 6-8.
Variation: If using canned beans, no need to steam them. If using frozen beans, prepare according to directions on package, but cook 3 minutes less than instructions indicate.

G-d blessed the Sabbath day with the blessings of each of the weekdays. He sanctified it with the sanctity of each of the holidays.
   This may be compared to the cook who prepares a special delicacy, seasoned with a taste of every good thing in the pantry!
(Rabbi Chanoch of Alexander)

Spicy Beans

1-1½ lb. (500-750 gm.) string beans
1 tsp. salt
½ tsp. basil
½ tsp. thyme (or allspice)

dash garlic powder
1 Tbsp. minced onion
¼ cup water
2 Tbsp. oil

Break string beans into 1-inch pieces. Put all ingredients into a medium-sized pot. Cover and cook over medium heat 20 minutes or until tender. Good hot or cold. Serves 6-8.

Even on the Sabbath a meal of greens accompanied by love of wife and family is preferable to a fine beef dinner with ill feeling. Thus, one should not buy extravagant delicacies if he fears it may anger his wife, or his parents.

(*Sefer Chasidim*)

Ratatouille

1 small eggplant	1½ tsp. salt
3-4 medium zucchini	1 cup thinly sliced onion
1 green pepper	3 medium tomatoes
⅓ cup olive oil	2 Tbsp. sugar
2 Tbsp. white vinegar	½ tsp. basil
2 cloves garlic, crushed	½ tsp. oregano

Peel eggplant, slice ³/₈-inches thick, cut into 3 by 1 inch strips. Trim ends of zucchini, cut into 1½ inch by ¼ inch by ¼ inch strips. Cut green pepper into strips. In bowl combine olive oil, vinegar, garlic and salt. In 3 quart casserole layer eggplant and zucchini. Drizzle in half of oil mixture. Top with onion and green pepper. Drizzle in rest of oil mixture. Cover, bake at 350° F (175° C) for 45 minutes. Peel and slice tomatoes. Arrange tomatoes on top of casserole, sprinkle with sugar, basil and oregano. Bake at 350° F (175° C) for 15 more minutes. Serve hot or cold. Serves 6 to 8.

Eggplant with Garlic Sauce

1 medium-large eggplant, sliced	1 tsp. salt
2-3 Tbsp. oil	2 Tbsp. sugar
2 tsp. ginger	2 Tbsp. vinegar
2 tsp. garlic powder	1 tsp. soy sauce
½ cup water	2 Tbsp. cornstarch + 3 Tbsp. water

Fry eggplant in oil until golden brown. With fork, gently press to squeeze out excess oil. Remove eggplant from pan and set aside. Leave about 1 Tbsp. oil in pan. Add ginger, garlic, water, salt, sugar, vinegar and soy sauce. Bring to a boil. Stir in cornstarch/water mixture and blend well. Add eggplant and mix thoroughly. Cook for a few more minutes until sauce is slightly thickened. Serve hot or cold. Serves 4-6.

The candle's flame is especially appropiate to the Sabbath. It is characteristic of a flame that can ignite many torches without being diminished in any way.

This is the special property of the Sabbath. It casts holiness upon all the other weekdays, yet its own sanctity is in no way lessened.

(Ben Ish Hai)

To eliminate bitterness from eggplant, slice eggplant and sprinkle each piece with a little salt. Let stand ½-hour. Press or squeeze out excess water. To fry: Blot dry with paper towel.

Scalloped Eggplant

1 large eggplant	1 green pepper
salt	1 medium can tomatoes
4 Tbsp. margarine	pepper
1 small onion, diced	seasoned bread crumbs

Peel and cube eggplant. Sprinkle with salt and let stand 30 minutes. Rinse and drain off liquid. Melt margarine, brown onions and green pepper. Add eggplant, tomatoes, salt and pepper to taste. Cook 15 minutes. Place mixture in shallow greased loaf pan, and sprinkle bread crumbs on top. Bake at 375° F (185° C) for 15-20 minutes. Serves 4-6.

Chopped Cabbage

1 medium-sized cabbage	1½ tsp. salt
1 onion, diced	juice of 1½ lemons
handful of raisins	¼ cup ketchup

Separate cabbage leaves. Check carefully. Chop leaves. Simmer cabbage in water which barely covers it for 10-15 minutes. Add remaining ingredients and cook on a low flame for ¾ hour until very soft.
Serves 6.

Sweet and Sour Red Cabbage

6 cups red cabbage, shredded	1½ Tbsp. flour
3 tart apples, sliced thinly	4 Tbsp. vinegar
½ onion, diced	2 Tbsp. sugar
1 tsp. salt	2 Tbsp. wine
1 cup water	2 Tbsp. oil

Separate cabbage leaves, check and shred. Cook cabbage, apple, onion, salt and water over low heat for 20 minutes. Make a paste with flour and vinegar, and add to cabbage. Add sugar, wine and oil. Taste. Add more wine, sugar or vinegar according to taste. Cook for ½ hour more on a low flame. Serve hot or cold. Serves 6-8.

Keep the Sabbath day to sanctify it, as the L-rd your G-d commanded you. Six days shall you labor and do all your work. But the seventh day is the Sabbath of the L-rd your G-d. On it you shall do no work, not you nor your son, daughter, slave, maidservant, ox, donkey, nor any of your animals, nor your stranger within your gates in order that your slave and maidservant rest as you do. And you shall remember that you were a slave in the land of Egypt and that the L-rd your G-d took you out of there with a mighty hand and outstretched arm. Therefore the L-rd your G-d commanded you to keep the Sabbath day.

(Deuteronomy 5)

Chinese Medley

1 head cabbage	1 tsp. salt
1 cup celery	$1/8$ tsp. pepper
1 green pepper	1 tsp. soy sauce
⅔ cup chopped onions	1 cup water
2 Tbsp. oil	

Separate cabbage leaves, check and shred. Cut celery diagonally into chunks. Cut green pepper into strips. Heat oil in large skillet. Add all the vegetables and stir-fry for 2 minutes. Remove from flame; add seasonings and water. Just before Shabbos, cover and reheat. Keep on covered flame (*blech*) where it won't overcook. (Vegetables should be crisp; they should not boil).

Beets in Thick Sauce

1 can sliced beets (or 2 cups cooked) with liquid	2 Tbsp. flour
1 large onion, sliced	dash pepper
2 Tbsp. margarine	salt, if needed

Sauté onion slices in margarine until transparent. Stir in flour until smooth. Add liquid to the mixture and stir until thickened. Pour in the sliced beets and stir. Taste and season. Beets are now ready to be kept warm until serving time. (Or refrigerate and reheat just before Shabbos).
(To cook fresh beets, wash them well, peel and slice. Cover the slices with salted water (about 2½ cups for 2 cups of beet slices). Bring to a boil and then reduce heat, cooking about 40 minutes till fork-tender. Liquid will reduce. Use all of it for this recipe).

Duchess Potatoes

2 cups cooked potatoes	1 egg white
2 egg yolks	paprika

Mash potatoes and add beaten egg yolks. Form into balls and arrange on a greased baking sheet. Brush with lightly beaten egg white, sprinkle with paprika, and brown in a hot oven. Serve hot. Serves 6.

Spicy Oven-Fried Potatoes

6 potatoes
½ cup oil
1-2 Tbsp. garlic powder

3-4 Tbsp. paprika
1-2 Tbsp. salt

Peel potatoes and cut into large pieces. Mix paprika and garlic with oil. Coat each piece of potato with oil mixture. Arrange on baking sheet. Sprinkle with salt. Bake at 400° F (200° C) for 1½-hours. Serve hot. Serves 6.
Variation: Pour 1 cup water onto baking sheet for a moister version.

Country Fried Potatoes

6 potatoes, boiled
2 onions
3 Tbsp. margarine or oil
1 tsp. salt

¼ tsp. pepper
dash paprika
dried parsley

Slice cold boiled potatoes. Melt margarine or oil in skillet. Fry sliced onions until brown. Add potatoes. Season with salt, pepper and paprika. Brown on both sides. Sprinkle with parsley. Serve warm on Friday night.

If potatoes are soaked in salt water for 20 minutes before baking, they will bake more rapidly.

Spanish Rice

1 carrot, diced
1 onion, diced
1 green or red pepper, diced
2 Tbsp. olive oil
1 cup brown rice
1 ripe tomato

¼ cup tomato paste
2½ cups water (approximately)
salt
pepper
oregano

Sauté diced vegetables in oil until tender. Check rice and rinse. Add rice and sauté until dry. Blend tomato and add to tomato paste. Add enough water to make 2 cups of liquid. Add spices and liquid to rice and bring to a boil. Do not stir! Cover and simmer on very low heat until all water is absorbed. Serve hot. Serves 4.

Reheat cooked rice in a heavy pan with a tight lid. Sprinkle water over the rice using about 2 tablespoons of water to each cup of rice. Cover and place over a low heat until hot, about 5-10 minutes. Or, place rice in a double boiler and heat over hot water for 10 minutes.

73

Vegetable Fried Rice

1 cup raw rice
2½ cups boiling water
1 green pepper, coarsely chopped
2 onions, coarsely chopped
½ lb. (250 gm.) mushrooms, sliced

3 Tbsp. oil
2 eggs
2 firm tomatoes, diced
½ cup shelled fresh peas (optional)
2 Tbsp. soy sauce

Check rice and rinse. Cook rice in water in covered pot until water is absorbed, about 20-30 minutes. Sauté peppers, onions and mushrooms in oil. Scramble the eggs until dry, stirring constantly. Add vegetables and eggs to rice mixture. Refrigerate. Before Shabbos, add tomatoes, peas and soy sauce. Heat, covered at 350° F (175° C) for 20 minutes. Serve hot. Serves 6.

Fried Rice

Over one hundred years ago the first Shabbos afternoon Tehillim group was organized in the Old City of Jerusalem. Since then, these children's groups have proliferated and exist in many parts of the world. What they all have in common is the singing of King David's Psalms. If you don't have a Tehillim group in your neighborhood, why not organize one?

1 cup rice
2 cups water
2 onions, diced
oil
salt to taste

pepper to taste
paprika to taste
2 cloves garlic
2 eggs

Cook rice in water over medium flame until water is absorbed. Fry onions in oil until light brown. Add seasonings. Mix rice and onions together. Add eggs one at a time. Mix very well, until uniform in color. Taste and season. Keep warm in frying pan or double boiler. Serve hot. Serves 4.

Farfel Side Dish

1½ cups farfel (egg barley)
1 cup diced onions
chicken fat, oil or margarine

chicken soup or water
2 tsp. salt
dash pepper

Fry onion until golden in chicken fat, oil or margarine. Add the farfel and fry on a low flame until fat is absorbed. Add liquid to cover plus 1 cup more and cook until farfel swells to absorb liquid. Add salt and pepper to taste. Serve hot. Serves 6.

Vegetable Strudel

½ cup spinach, shredded
½ cup squash, shredded
½ cup cabbage, shredded
½ cup eggplant, shredded
½ cup tomatoes, shredded
½ cup onions, shredded
salt to taste

pepper to taste
2-3 Tbsp. oil
2 Tbsp. cold water
2 Tbsp. flour
4 Tbsp. wheat germ
1 recipe flaky pastry dough (p. 119)
sesame seed (optional)

Check spinach and cabbage well. All vegetables should be shredded or finely cut. Any vegetable may be substituted for another except the cabbage. Rinse vegetables and steam in tightly covered pot over low heat with only the water which clings to them from rinsing. When tender, season with salt and pepper and add 1 Tbsp. oil. Mix together water and flour until smooth and stir in lightly, shaking pot to prevent sticking. Cook over low heat 3-4 minutes longer. Cool and spread on dough that has been sprinkled lightly with wheat germ. Roll as for strudel. Sprinkle with sesame seeds. Cut and bake at 375° F (185° C) for 20 minutes, until browned. Serve warm. Makes 10 servings.

Keep a toothbrush in the kitchen to clean beaters, graters, choppers and other utensils.

The Sabbath candles radiate peace.
(*Sefer Hamidos LeMaharan*)

Vegetable Loaf

1 cup chopped onion
1 cup chopped celery
1 cup grated carrots
1 cup ground walnuts
2-3 Tbsp. oil

1 cup breadcrumbs
2 eggs
1 tsp. seasonings, to taste
1 boullion cube dissolved in
1 cup hot water

Sauté the vegetables and walnuts in oil for 15 minutes. Add remaining ingredients. Pour into oiled loaf pan. Bake at 350° F (175° C) for 45 minutes. Delicious served hot with gravy; also good cold. Serves 8.

"Remember the Sabbath day to keep it holy." (Exodus 20) How do you keep it holy? — By learning Torah and Mishnah, by feasting, by wearing new clothes, and by resting.
(*Tana d've Eliyahu*)

Once upon a time, a wealthy man became poor. He was so poor that he had to travel from village to village begging for his bread. On his travels he once found himself on a mountain whose stones were very pleasing to his eye. He filled his sack with the pretty stones and continued on his way. The stones, however, were heavy, especially for a tired and hungry man, so one by one he discarded them.

When he reached a village, he approached the house of a poor teacher. The man searched in his sack for a coin to offer the teacher, but all his hand found was a stone. The teacher's face lit up when he saw the beautiful stone and assured the poor man that this stone would be his salvation. Almost against his will the teacher led the man to the house of a dealer of precious stones. The dealer imme-

Stuffed Peppers

¾ cup tomato purée	raisins
5 cups water	6-8 medium-sized peppers
2 Tbsp. lemon juice	¾ cup raw rice
3 Tbsp. brown or white sugar	2 onions, diced and fried
2 tsp. salt	

Combine tomato purée, water, lemon juice, sugar, 1 tsp. salt and raisins in a medium pot. Bring to a boil and simmer while preparing peppers. Combine rice, onion, and 1 tsp. salt. Cut off tops of peppers and stuff three-quarters full. Place peppers upright in sauce. Cook on a low flame for 1 hour. Baste frequently. Make sure there is enough liquid. Add water if necessary. Serve hot. Serves 6-8.
Variation: Combine 1 lb. (450 gm.) chopped meat, 1 tsp. garlic powder and 1 or 2 eggs with raw rice.

Curried Apples and Celery

2 Tbsp. margarine	1 Tbsp. flour
2 cups celery, sliced diagonally	1 tsp. curry powder
1 small onion, sliced thin	½ tsp. salt
2 small apples, peeled & diced	⅛ tsp. pepper

Sauté celery and onion in margarine for 10 minutes, stirring occasionally. Add apples. Cover and cook 5 minutes more. Gently stir in remaining ingredients, and remove from fire until just before Shabbos. Reheat and keep warm on covered flame (*blech*). Serves 6.

Chick Peas (Arbes)

1 lb. (500 gm.) chick peas	pepper
salt	

Soak chick peas for at least 8 hours. Rinse and check. Boil for 30 minutes or longer until tender in water to cover plus 2 cups. Check water level occasionally to prevent burning. Drain. Season with salt and pepper to taste.
Variation: Marinated chick peas: After cooking as above, marinate overnight in ½-1 cup of French dressing (p.89) or marinade for vegetables (p.87).

Knishes

2½ cups sifted flour	⅔ cup salad oil
1 tsp. baking powder	2 Tbsp. water
½ tsp. salt	Filling: see below
2 eggs	

Sift flour, baking powder and salt together in a bowl. Make a well in the center and drop the eggs, oil and water into it. Work them into the flour mixture by hand or electric mixer and knead until smooth.

To fill: Divide dough into 2 and roll as thinly as possible. Brush with oil. Spread the filling on 1 side of the dough and roll like a jelly roll. Cut into 1½-inch slices and lay them on oiled baking sheet. Or, cut rolled dough into 3-inch circles. Place a tablespoon of filling on each circle, draw the edges together and pinch firmly. Place on oiled baking sheet. Bake at 375° F (185° C) for 35 minutes, or until browned. Makes about 24 knishes. To prevent sogginess, keep warm in uncovered pan.

Mushroom Filling

1 cup diced raw onions	1 cup water or liquid from mushrooms
3 Tbsp. margarine	salt
2 cups canned mushrooms without liquid	pepper
3 Tbsp. flour	

Sauté onion in margarine until transparent. Drain mushrooms, reserving liquid, and sauté with onion until golden brown. Stir in flour until smooth, add salt and pepper to taste. Gradually stir in water or liquid drained from mushrooms and cook, stirring until bubbly and thickened.

Potato Filling

1 cup chopped onion	1 egg, beaten
6 Tbsp. chicken fat or margarine	1 tsp. salt
2 cups mashed potatoes	¼ tsp. pepper

Brown onions in fat or margarine. Beat in the potatoes, egg, salt and pepper until fluffy.

Serving suggestion: Serve potato knishes with mushroom sauce, see p. 23.

diately ufte l the man 1,000 gold coins for the stone.

Flabbergasted, the poor man stood mute in wonder. The dealer, who construed the silence as hesitation to accept the offer, doubled his offer to 2,000 gold coins.

The poor man finally understood the worth of what he had — and the worth of what he had lost. He fell to the earth in tears, lamenting the many large, beautiful stones that he had thrown away.

So it is with man after he dies. Even if he possesses only one small mitzvah, that of having polished his shoes in honor of Shabbos, he will be rewarded handsomely for that good deed. But he will also regret all the many important good deeds that he forfeited during his lifetime.

(Apter Rav)

Salads, Dressings and Relishes

"Tasters of the Sabbath merit life."

How can we take maximum advantage of this principle on a weekly basis? By relishing the taste of all foods prepared for the Sabbath. Every individual seated at the table should be encouraged to sample each dish — thus increasing his merit as taster-of-the-Sabbath.

A practical way to add variety to Sabbath menus is to prepare some salads, pickled vegetables, or relishes. As mentioned in our Preface, all food preparations should be done before the Sabbath. Therefore, we have chosen salads for this section which can be made in advance. If parve utensils are used, these become flexible additions to any of the Sabbath meals.

Russian Salad

3 onions, sliced	1 tsp. salt
5 red peppers, cut in strips	1 bay leaf
8-10 carrrots, shredded	½ tsp. oregano
3 tomatoes, sliced	½ tsp. basil
1 Tbsp. oil	1 tsp. sugar

Layer the onions, peppers and carrots in a large pot with 1 Tbsp. oil in the bottom. Make layers of each, then slice tomatoes on top. Add seasonings. Cook over very low heat, covered, for about 1½ hours. Serve cold.

Corn and Pepper Salad

2 ears corn	salt
2 small red sweet peppers	1 black olive

Cook ears of corn until tender. Strip kernels from cobs, add finely chopped sweet pepper. Add salt, mix and top with black olive. Serves 2 as salad, or up to eight as relish.

Potato Salad

5-6 medium potatoes	2 tsp. salt
1 green pepper, diced (optional)	½ tsp. pepper
1 stalk celery, diced (optional)	mayonnaise to taste
1 cup canned peas and carrots	¼ cup pickle juice
3-4 pickles, diced	paprika for garnish

Cook potatoes in jackets. Peel and cube them. Mix in remaining ingredients. Sprinkle with paprika.

Old-Fashioned Potato Salad

½ cup mayonnaise
½ cup minced onion
1 Tbsp. white vinegar
1 tsp. salt
⅛ tsp. pepper

1 hard boiled egg, chopped
1½ lbs. (¾ kg.) potatoes, cooked
   and cubed (about 3 cups)
1 cup thinly sliced celery

Mix mayonnaise, onion, vinegar, salt, pepper and egg in a medium-sized bowl. Add potatoes and celery. Toss to coat well. Cover and chill at least 4 hours.

"Its tasters merit life."
One should sample every
dish prepared for the Sabbath before the candles
are lit to ensure that everything is perfectly seasoned.
(Mishnah Berurah)

Marinated Potato Salad

4 large potatoes, peeled
⅔ cup oil
¾ cup vinegar
1½ tsp. salt

½ tsp. pepper
½ onion
1 green pepper
2 Tbsp. parsley

Slice the potatoes very thinly and place them in a saucepan with next 4 ingredients (no water!). Bring to a boil. Lower heat and cook about 20 minutes, till slices are tender. Chill. Before Shabbos, add a ½ onion chopped fine and a green pepper cut in thin strips. Sprinkle with snipped parsley.

Russian Potato Salad

5 large potatoes
2 medium beets
3 large carrots

2 medium onions
5 pickles
4-5 Tbsp. mayonnaise

Boil potatoes, beets and carrots together. Cool and peel. Shred coarsely. Dice onions and pickles finely. Add mayonnaise. Mix and serve cold.

Salads are more inviting when decorated attractively. Thin slices of peppers, tomatoes, cucumbers, radishes, carrots and olives – green or black – can be used to add eye appeal.

Tangy Beet Salad

5-6 cooked beets
3 raw carrots
4 pickles

1½ tsp. salt
2 tsp. sugar
mayonnaise

Shred beets and carrots. Chop pickles. Add salt and sugar. Add mayonnaise to taste.

Quick Beet Relish

3 medium beets, scrubbed and peeled
2 Tbsp. sugar

¼ cup. vinegar

Clean beets and boil until tender, about 30 minutes. Peel and shred. Mix sugar and vinegar. Pour over beets. Keeps for at least 2 weeks.

Shopping for the Sabbath, one should say with every purchase, "I am buying this in honor of the Sabbath."

(Ari)

Moroccan Beet Salad

6 small beets
2 small onions, chopped
2 tsp. cumin
salt

pepper
juice from ½ lemon or
    ¼ cup vinegar

Scrub beets; cut off tops. Cook whole beets until tender. Drain and let cool; remove skins. Cut into small strips or cubes. Add finely chopped onion. Add seasonings and liquid.

"And you shall call the Sabbath a delight." (Isaiah 58). How does one show this delight? Rabbi Judah son of Rabbi Samuel ben Shilath said in Rav's name: With a dish of beets, large fish and heads of garlic. Rabbi Hiyya ben Ashi said in Rav's name: Any dish however small, if it is prepared in honor of the Sabbath is considered a delight.

(Talmud Bavli)

Beet Nut Salad

3 medium beets
1½ cups pineapple, drained
½ cup walnuts, broken

juice of ½ lemon
sugar to taste

Cook beets and shred. Cut up pineapple or use crushed pineapple. Combine the shredded beets, pineapple and nuts. Add lemon juice and sugar to taste. Chill.

Variation: Use raw beets.

Cucumber Salad

4 large cucumbers, unpeeled	2 Tbsp. vinegar or lemon juice
2 tsp. salt	3 Tbsp. sugar
1 medium onion, sliced	

Wash cucumbers, slice thinly and sprinkle with salt. Let stand 15 minutes, then drain well. Add remaining of ingredients. Taste and adjust seasonings as desired. Refrigerate.

Sweet and Sour Cukes

3 medium cucumbers (do not peel)	1 Tbsp. chopped parsley
½ cup cider vinegar	¼ tsp. ground pepper
¼ cup honey	½ tsp. salt

Score and slice the cucumbers very thinly. Place in a clear jar. Combine remaining ingredients and pour over cucumbers. Refrigerate overnight.

Carrot Salad

6-7 carrots	½ can diced pineapple
3 Tbsp. lemon juice	⅓ cup raisins
4 Tbsp. sugar	

Peel and shred carrots. Combine remaining ingredients.

Moroccan Carrot Salad

10 medium carrots	pepper
cumin	1 Tbsp. salad oil
juice from ½ lemon	parsley
salt	sweet paprika

Cut carrots into ¼-inch rounds. Cook in water to cover until tender, about 20 minutes. Drain and flavor with the listed seasonings and oil. Sprinkle with finely chopped parsley and sweet paprika for color.

Rabbi Elimelech of Lizensk was known for the special air of sanctity which filled his home in anticipation of the Sabbath. There was a very old woman who in her youth had been a servant girl in Rabbi Elimelech's house. When asked for anecdotes from the life of the great rabbi, she said, "One thing stays in my mind. During the week there were all sorts of quarrels in the kitchen, as is customary among servants. But each Friday afternoon, something came over us. We would fall upon one another and plead: 'My dear, please forgive me for all I did to you during the week.'"

(*Yaina shel Torah*)

Marinated Carrots

1 lb. (½ kg.) sliced carrots
1 onion, sliced into rings
1 green pepper, cut into strips

½ cup oil
½ cup vinegar
¼ cup sugar

Cook the carrots until tender. Put into a serving bowl with onion and pepper. Combine the oil, vinegar and sugar. Pour over the vegetables and marinate in the refrigerator for at least 1 day.

Bean Salad

1 cup cooked (or canned)
  kidney beans
1 cup cooked split peas
  (or canned peas)
1 cup cooked (or canned)
  string beans
1 cup cooked (or canned)
  wax beans
1 cup diced onion
½ cup chopped celery

½ cup chopped green pepper
½ cup chopped pimento (gamba)
1 cup oil
2 cups vinegar
1 cup sugar
1 tsp. salt (or more,
  to taste)
½ tsp. pepper
2 Tbsps. fresh dill stems,
  snipped

Combine all the ingredients in a large bowl. This salad can be made in advance. It keeps well for 3 weeks. You may substitute canned corn kernels, cooked lima beans, or whatever is available, for the recommended beans.

Honoring the Sabbath is preferable to a thousand fasts, for honoring the Sabbath derives from the Torah, while voluntary fasts are of Rabbinic origin.
(Midrash Tanhuma)

Cole Slaw

1 medium head cabbage
2 large carrots
1 green pepper, diced (optional)
1½-2 tsp. salt

3 Tbsp. sugar
3 Tbsp. lemon juice or vinegar,
  or both combined
mayonnaise

Clean and check cabbage leaves thoroughly. Shred cabbage and carrots. Combine with remaining ingredients, using enough mayonnaise to bind salad together. Chill.

If one sees a fine object during the week suitable for the Sabbath and doubts whether or not he can afford it, he should buy it and save it for the Sabbath as it is proper to thus honor the Sabbath. One should continuously honor the Sabbath this way all week long. The Creator will then show kindness to him and provide for all his needs in abundance. As he opens his hand for the Sabbath, so shall the heavens open for him and bless him with ample sustenance.
(Seder Ha-yom)

Cabbage Salad

1 head cabbage
2 cucumbers, thinly sliced
3 carrots, thinly sliced
1 large onion, thinly sliced

MARINADE:
½ cup vinegar
½ cup sugar
¼ cup oil
4 Tbsp. water
1½ tsp. salt

Check cabbage leaves and then shred. Mix vegetables together. Mix marinade ingredients together and pour over vegetables. Tastes delicious if made early in the week.
Variation: Add pieces of herring.

One way to wilt cabbage, so that it can be separated into whole leaves, is to freeze the whole head a few days in advance. 24 hours before you need the leaves, remove the head from freezer and allow it to defrost in a colander in the sink.

Kohlrabi Slaw

2 kohlrabi
1-2 carrots
½ green pepper
4 Tbsp. mayonnaise

2 Tbsp. vinegar or lemon juice
2 Tbsp. sugar
garlic powder

Shred kohlrabi and carrots. Cut green pepper into strips. Combine mayonnaise, vinegar, sugar and garlic powder. Taste and adjust seasonings if necessary. Pour over vegetables and toss.

Hot Pepper Salad

Singing the praises of the Almighty is especially appropriate for the Sabbath. As it is written: "A psalm, a song for the Sabbath day. It is good to give thanks to the Lord and to sing to Your name, Most High." (Tehillim 92)
(*Ohr HaShabbos*)

2 sweet peppers
2 tomatoes
1 hot pepper
¼ cup water

1 tsp. cumin
2 Tbsp. lemon juice
salt
pepper

Cut tomatoes into cubes, peppers into small strips and hot pepper into very tiny pieces. Put in frying pan with water. Cover and cook over a very low flame until very soft. Drain. Flavor with lemon juice, cumin, salt and pepper to taste. This salad is just as good without the hot pepper. Try it both ways. When first using hot pepper, be sure to use a very small amount until you get used to it.

Turkish Salad (a relish)

1 Tbsp. oil
2 lbs. (1 kg.) sweet red peppers
1 or 2 hot peppers
2 tomatoes

1 large onion
3 cloves garlic
1 tsp. salt
½ tsp. cumin

Finely chop all the vegetables and sauté in oil over low flame for 15 minutes. Add seasonings and more salt and cumin according to taste. Serve warm or cold. Keeps well in refrigerator.

Celery Root Salad

1-2 large celery roots
4 Tbsp. mayonnaise

1½ tsp. salt
juice of 1 lemon

Peel and grate celery root. Pour mayonnaise, salt and lemon juice over celery root. Adjust seasonings to taste.

Green Salad

½ cup cooked or canned peas
1 onion, chopped
4 stalks celery, chopped

3 Tbsps. mayonnaise
salt
pepper

Drain peas. Combine with remaining ingredients and season to taste.

Radish Salad

1 cup grated or finely chopped radish
1 hot pepper, minced (optional)
½ cup raw peas
½ cup raw string beans
¾ cup cucumber, in chunks
¼-½ cup cashew nutmeats (optional)

DRESSING:
½ cup oil
3-4 Tbsps. prepared tehina
1 tsp. soy sauce
1 clove garlic, crushed
2 Tbsp. lemon juice
salt to taste

Combine salad ingredients. Combine dressing ingredients. Then toss all together.

Help those who on the seventh day rest from plowing and harvesting, who walk slowly, who eat three meals in order to bless You. May their righteousness shine like the light of the seven days of Creation.

(Zemiroth)

To peel garlic, slice each clove in two down the center - the peel will pop off.

Waldorf Salad

2 large apples (tart)
1 cup celery stalks, diced
½ cup mayonnaise

2 Tbsp. coarsely chopped walnuts
salt
lemon juice

Cube apples with peel. Add celery and mayonnaise. Mix well. Season with salt and lemon juice to taste. Mix in chopped nuts.

Eggplant Salad

... And certainly it is necessary to clean the house of dust and dirt before the Sabbath in honor of the Sabbath. Imagine if a mortal king were to lodge at one's home how much effort one would expend to clean the house and arrange the furniture. All the more so for the Sabbath Queen.

(*Mishnah Berurah*)

3 large eggplants
3 Tbsp. lemon juice
1½ tsp. salt

1 tsp. garlic powder
2-3 Tbsp. mayonnaise

Wash eggplants very well. Pierce each one with a fork in a few places. Wrap each one in silver foil and place directly over fire to char for about 15 minutes until soft. Cool eggplants and peel under running water. Mash with a fork (or in food processor). Add lemon juice and seasonings to taste and mayonnaise.
Variation: Replace mayonnaise with ¼ cup tehina. Add 1-2 tsp. cumin to taste.

Marinated Eggplant Salad

3 medium eggplants
oil
salt
4 cloves garlic, crushed
2 tsp. paprika

½ cup vinegar
½ cup water
pinch sugar
1 onion, sliced

Honoring the Torah and honoring the Sabbath bring wealth.

(*Sefer Hamidos Le-Moharan*)

Choose long, lightweight eggplants. Remove both ends of each eggplant. Wash well, but do not peel. Slice into 1-inch (2.5 cm.) slices. Lay the slices on a cookie sheet and salt each one well on both sides. Allow to "sweat" for about an hour. Then rinse and pat dry. If possible, leave slices in a warm place (traditionally, in the sun) for several hours to become very dry. Fry a few slices at a time in hot oil, browning (but not burning!) on each side. Drain slightly and put slices in a large bowl. Add crushed garlic, paprika, vinegar, water, sugar and onion. Toss lightly. Keeps well in refrigerator for a week or more.

Marinade for Vegetables

1 cup oil
¾ cup wine vinegar
  or ¼ cup vinegar +
  ½ cup lemon juice
½ tsp. salt (or to taste)
pepper to taste
2 medium cloves garlic, minced

small amounts of dried herbs:
  marjoram
  thyme
  basil
  dill
  tarragon
  parsley
  oregano
  chives

Combine all ingredients. Pour over vegetables and marinate for at least a few hours. Try with steamed green beans and fresh thinly sliced onions. Garnish with sliced hard-boiled eggs, tomatoes and olives. Or use any cooked or canned vegetables, or combination, adding fresh vegetables according to your fancy.

*Eating the Sabbath
meals is like eating manna.
(Likutey Halachoth)*

Pickles

3 lbs. (1½ kg.) small cucumbers
2-3 Tbsp. coarse salt
1 bunch fresh dill
10 cloves garlic, peeled

1 Tbsp. vinegar (or more, to taste)
2 Tbsp. mixed pickling spice
  (peppercorns, bay leaves, dill seeds)

Wash cucumbers well and keep them in cold water in the refrigerator until you are ready to pickle them. Do this a day in advance for a crisper pickle.
Pour boiling water into a 2-quart (2-liter) glass or plastic jar, pouring some over lid as well. This is to kill any bacteria which could spoil the pickles. Then pour water out. Pour salt into jar and add some boiling water to dissolve it. Check dill carefully for insects and wrap it in cloth. Put dill and garlic into jar. Then pack in the cucumbers, standing up, as tightly as possible. Add the vinegar and spice and fill the jar with tap water, almost to the top, being sure to cover all the pickles. Close the jar tightly and invert briefly to mix the brine. Stand the jar on a sunny windowsill. In 2 summer days or 4 winter days, as a rule, your pickles will be ready. Experiment with half-sour timing according to your family's taste.

*The concept of holiness
appears first in the Torah
with reference to the Sabbath day. This is to teach
us that the Sabbath is the
root and foundation of all
holiness in the world.
(Be'er Mosheh)*

Zuke Pickles

3 medium zucchini, very
   thinly sliced
2 Tbsp. diced onion
½ cup vinegar

1½ tsp. salt
dash pepper
½ cup water

Combine in a medium-sized container. Cover and refrigerate. Serves 6.

Instant Pickle Slices

A way to make the Sabbath a festive day for the littlest tots is to get each one a toy which is set aside for the Sabbath. While others are busily preparing for the Sabbath, your little one can do his part by putting away toys not suitable for the Sabbath and taking down that "just-for-Shabbos" one. After havdala when clean-up operations are on, his special job can be setting this toy aside once more till the Sabbath Queen returns.

10 cucumbers
1½ cups vinegar
3½ cups water
2 Tbsp. salt

4 tsp. sugar
1 sliced onion
3-4 cloves garlic (optional)

Wash and slice (do not peel) cucumbers. Mix remaining ingredients in a medium-sized pot. Add cucumbers and bring to a boil for 5 minutes, until color changes to light green. Let cool. Refrigerate. Pickling juice can be reused for another batch. *Variation:* Add carrot and red pepper, thinly sliced, before cooking.

Pickled Peppers

2 lbs. (1 kg.) green peppers
2 Tbsp. sugar
1 Tbsp. salt

½-1 cup vinegar, to taste
2-3 cloves garlic

Remove stems and seeds from peppers and cut in halves or quarters. Place in stainless steel pot with water to cover and bring to a boil. Simmer on low flame 15-20 minutes, stirring occasionally, until color changes. Pour off water leaving ¼ cup hot water. Melt sugar and salt in the reserved hot water. Arrange peppers in a covered container. Add salt/sugar mixture and vinegar to cover. Crush and add garlic. Taste and adjust seasoning. Refrigerate. Keeps at least 2 weeks.

Horseradish (Chrein)

¼ lb. (100 gm.) horseradish root
   peeled and cut into chunks
1-3 medium sized cooked beets
1-1½ tsp. salt

2-3 tsp. sugar
2 Tbsp. vinegar
2-3 Tbsp. beet water

Place all ingredients in food processor, or blender, and grind to desired consistency. The more beets you use, the milder the flavor.

Mayonnaise

2 eggs
1 tsp. salt
dash pepper
2 Tbsp. vinegar

1 tsp. mustard or
   3 heaping tsp. prepared mustard
2 Tbsp. lemon juice
2 cups vegetable oil

Place eggs in food processor or blender and blend 2 minutes. Add seasonings. Blend. Slowly pour in oil, a little at a time, while machine is running. Increase oil until mayonnaise is firm. Taste. Add seasonings if necessary.

It is written in our holy writings that one should repent and examine one's deeds every Friday. The Sabbath is called the Queen and it is as though one were receiving royalty. Certainly one must not greet royalty dressed in rags stained with the filth of sins.

(Mishnah Berurah)

French Dressing

½ cup sugar
¼ cup vinegar
1 Tbsp. lemon juice
2 Tbsp. ketchup

½ cup oil
1 tsp. salt
1 tsp. paprika
1 small onion

Combine all the above in blender jar. Blend at high speed until smooth.

Russian Dressing

½ cup mayonnaise
⅓ cup ketchup
garlic powder

paprika
snipped parsley

Combine in a bowl, adding some water if desired.

Combine some of each of the following in a salt shaker for your own salad seasoning:

   oregano
   marjoram
   thyme
   savory
   basil
   rosemary
   sage

Desserts

After a warm and nourishing festive meal the family and guests continue to discuss Torah and sing the praises of the day. Before the beverages and baked goods, something light, creamy or fruity may be just the thing.

Should neighbors or additional guests drop in, the mistress of the house may wish to set out some small treats which could be eaten in honor of the Sabbath, even after a satisfying feast.

Applesauce

6 tart apples	**⅓ cup sugar**
⅓ cup water	**½ tsp. cinnamon**

Peel, core and quarter apples. Place in ice cold water to prevent discoloration. Cook covered in ⅓ cup water for 30 minutes or until soft. Add sugar and cinnamon and stir. Simmer 5 minutes longer. When cool, mash with a spoon. Makes about 3 cups, serving 4-5.

Baked Apples

6 baking apples	**½ tsp. cinnamon**
¼-½ cup sugar	**water**

Wash apples. Core two-thirds of the way down. Arrange in a baking dish, or in a muffin tin to keep shape better. Mix sugar and cinnamon. Fill each apple with mixture. Cover bottom of pan with ¼ inch (.5 cm.) water. Bake at 375° F (185° C) for 45 minutes. Baste after 30 minutes. Cool. Remove apples. Boil remaining syrup until thick and pour over apples.

Variation: Fill apples with brown sugar and/or add raisins.

Wintry treat: For Friday night's dessert, keep freshly baked apples warm (on covered flame) with the other food.

Pear Compote

6 pears	**½ cup sugar**
1 cup water	**5 cloves**

Peel, core and quarter pears, placing in ice cold water to prevent discoloration during preparation. Bring water and sugar to boil. Add pears and cloves. Simmer 20 minutes or longer until tender. Remove cloves. Serves 6.

Variation: Peel, core and cut pears in halves. Add ½ cup red wine and 1 tsp. lemon juice to liquid.

A few drops of food coloring gives coconut a special look. In a jar, place ⅓ cup flaked coconut and a few drops of coloring. Cover and shake well.

Fruits Refraichis

variety of fruit in season	**shredded coconut or ground nuts**
wine or cognac	**candied cherries or fresh**
lemon juice	**strawberries**
sugar	

Pare and cube fruit. Mix each 3 cups of fruit with ¼ cup wine or cognac. Add lemon juice and sugar to taste. Chill. Serve in individual dishes. Sprinkle shredded coconut or nuts over each serving and top with a cherry or strawberry.

Lemon Cream

8 eggs, separated	**juice of 2 lemons**
½ cup margarine	**grated rind of 1 lemon**
½ cup sugar	

Combine egg yolks, margarine, sugar and lemon juice in the top of a double boiler. Cook over hot water (just below the boiling point), stirring constantly until thick and creamy. Be careful not to overheat. Transfer mixture to a mixing bowl and beat until foamy. Beat egg whites until stiff and fold into the yolk mixture. Mix in the grated rind. Pour into 6 custard cups. Refrigerate. Serves 6.

Variation: Pour the mixture into a casserole dish lined with waxed paper. Place the dish on a trivet in a pan of hot water and bake at 300° F (150° C) for 1½ hours. To unmold, loosen custard and turn the casserole upside down. Let it stand until the custard unmolds itself. Serve cold. Serves 6.

To get more juice out of lemons and other citrus fruits, keep them at room temperature. If a lemon is hard, roll it on a hard surface until it softens or place in hot water for a few minutes.

Brandied Orange Dessert

5 oranges
½ cup chopped toasted almonds
¾ cup chopped dates

⅔ cup orange juice
⅓ cup brandy

Peel oranges and cut in half, lengthwise. Slice thin half-rounds. Toss orange slices with other ingredients. Chill at least 2 hours.

Parve Ice Cream

6 eggs, separated
1 cup sugar
½ cup oil
2 tsp. cocoa

1 tsp. instant coffee powder
1 tsp. vanilla
raisins (optional)

Put yolks, oil and flavoring into blender. Blend well. Beat whites with sugar until stiff. Fold together carefully. Add raisins. Freeze.
Variation: 1. Omit cocoa and coffee. Add grated lemon peel and ½ cup coconut.
2. Omit cocoa and coffee. Add ¾ cup fresh strawberries, ¾ cup cooked or canned peaches or ¾ cup cooked or canned apricots.

Walk during the week when you can drive? Who would so such a thing? Fortunately, the Sabbath affords us the opportunity to stroll at leisure with our families. We can explore nearby parks, reserves or neighborhoods we would never get to during the week.

Coconut Ice Cream

6 eggs, separated
¾ cup sugar
½ cup oil

4 oz (100 gm.) shredded coconut
2 tsp. vanilla

Beat egg whites with sugar until stiff. In another bowl, beat egg yolks with oil, then add coconut and vanilla. Fold in egg whites. Freeze. Remix by hand after 1½ hours and refreeze. Serves 10.
Variation: Decrease sugar to ½ cup. Break 4 oz. (100 gm.) bittersweet chocolate into pieces with food processor or blender and add to yolk mixture.

Layered Lemon and Coffee Ice Cream

12 eggs, separated
2 cups sugar
2 tsp. vanilla

¾-1 cup oil
1 Tbsp. instant coffee
2 fresh lemons

Beat whites stiff. Add the sugar and beat again. Fold in yolks. Add the vanilla and oil gently. Divide the mixture in half. Add the coffee (dissolved in 1 Tbsp. hot water if you prefer) to half the mixture. Spread in a 9 by 13 inch pan and freeze. Then, squeeze the lemon juice into the other half and refrigerate the mixture. After about an hour spread the lemon mixture over the coffee part and cover the whole thing well. Freeze. (Optional: Sprinkle with toasted nuts or coconut. Top each portion with a maraschino cherry). Serve in squares. Serves 12-20.

Strawberry Ice

1 egg white (room temperature)
½ lb. (250 gm.) strawberries

½ cup sugar
⅛ tsp. lemon juice

Beat egg white with beater. Mix hulled strawberries, sugar and lemon juice in blender. Add gradually to egg white and beat for 10-15 minutes. Increases greatly in volume. Freeze. Serves 6-8.

When one visits a friend on Sabbath morning, he should not greet him with "good morning," as he does during the week but rather with "*Shabbat shalom*" or "good Shabbos" to fulfill the *mitzvah* of remembering the Sabbath.

(*Shelah*)

The Sabbath reunites body and soul because physical gratification and enjoyment enter the realm of *mitzvah*. The struggle between the spiritual and the physical ceases on the day of rest. The Sabbath is the great peacemaker between body and soul; therefore we say "*Shabbat shalom*."

(*Ben Ish Hai*)

94

Burnt Almond Ice Cream

¾ **cup brown sugar**	**4 eggs**
½ **cup water**	**1 tsp. vanilla**
5 oz. (150 gm.) margarine	½ **cup almonds**

Heat brown sugar with water until bubbly. Whip margarine, eggs and vanilla in blender or food processor. Add hot brown sugar mixture and blend well until mixture is very smooth. Freeze. Bake almonds for 10 minutes in a medium oven 350° F (175° C), stirring to prevent burning. Grind. Remove frozen mixture after 8-10 hours and thaw partially. Beat for 7-8 minutes with an electric mixer. Mixture should increase in volume. Mix in the toasted almonds. Refreeze. Serves 6-8.

Chocolate Mousse

5 oz. (150 gm.) parve chocolate	**3 Tbsp. confectioner's sugar**
4 eggs, separated	**2 Tbsp. wine**

Melt chocolate in double boiler. Beat egg yolks and add sugar, wine and melted chocolate. Beat egg whites and fold into egg yolk mixture. Spoon into parfait glasses. Top with parve whipped cream or nuts. Refrigerate.
Variation: Combine 8 oz. (250 gm.) cookie crumbs, ½ cup coconut and 4 oz. (100 gm.) soft margarine. Spread in a pie pan. Spoon mousse into shell. Refrigerate.

Chocolate Mousse Pie

1 cup sugar	**2 Tbsp. wine**
½ **cup flour**	**2 egg yolks, beaten**
2 Tbsp. cocoa	**2 Tbsp. margarine**
2 cups boiling water	**1 baked pie shell**
1 tsp. vanilla	

Combine sugar, flour and cocoa in a saucepan. Pour boiling water over the mixture. Add wine and vanilla. Cook over a low flame until thickened. Remove 2 Tbsp. of the mixture and mix with the egg yolks. Pour yolk mixture back into the boiling mixture and continue mixing. Add margarine. When melted, turn fire off. (Constant mixing is important since this can burn easily.) Pour into baked pie shell. Decorate with nuts or coconut.

Whoever delights in the Sabbath — all his wishes are granted.

(Talmud Bavli)

Give the term "Oneg Shabbos" special meaning for your older children, by preparing a treat to be served after a study session with the adults when younger children are asleep.

95

Frozen Mousse Pie

12 eggs, separated	2-3 tsp. rum or liqueur
1½ cups sugar	6 Tbsp. flour
1½ cups margarine	1 tsp. baking powder
14 oz. (350 gm.) chocolate	

Beat egg whites till frothy. Gradually add sugar and beat till stiff. Set aside. Place margarine and chocolate in a saucepan and cook until melted. Beat yolks in mixer. Add liqueur and chocolate-margarine mixture. Mix well. Fold egg whites into chocolate mixture thoroughly. Remove ¼ of the mixture and pour into a bowl for crust. Mix in 6 Tbsp. of flour and 1 tsp. baking powder. Place on bottom of 2 9-inch pie plates or 3 8-inch pie plates. Bake for 15-20 minutes in a medium oven. It should be dry and spongy. When cool, spoon the rest of the mousse over crust. Freeze and serve frozen. Wait for compliments!

Fancy Gel

1 package gel-dessert, any flavor	½ cup parve whippingcream
1½ cups boiling water	

Boil water; dissolve powder. Whip the parve cream and mix with gel until smooth. Refrigerate. Served in a mold, this is an attractive dessert. 4-6 servings.

Parve Peach Pleasure

6 ripe peaches, peeled	¼ cup sugar (more or less depending
3 eggs	on the sweetness of the fruit)
¼ cup oil	

Blend all ingredients in blender or food processor and freeze. For creamier texture, take out a few minutes before serving.
Variation: You may use a combination of peaches and apricots.

Oriental Fried Walnuts

4 cups shelled walnuts	oil
6 cups water	salt
½ cup sugar	

Bring water to a boil in a large saucepan. Add walnuts and heat again to the boiling point. Continue to cook for 1 minute. Pour into a colander and rinse under running hot water. Transfer walnuts into large bowl, add sugar and stir gently. Let mixture sit until sugar is dissolved (2 or 3 minutes). Meanwhile, dry saucepan well and pour in oil about 1 inch high. Heat the oil over a medium flame and fry the walnuts, half at a time, stirring till golden (about 5 minutes). Drain in colander. Sprinkle with salt, stirring to keep them from sticking together. Store in covered container. (May be made early in the week.)

Oatey Apple Chewies

½ cup margarine	3 cups quick rolled oats
2 cups sugar	1 cup chopped walnuts
2 Tbsp. flour	1 tsp. vanilla
¼ tsp. salt	ground nuts, sugar, cinnamon
1 cup grated apple	

Melt margarine in a heavy pan. Stir in sugar, flour, salt, and apples. Bring to a boil and keep boiling for 1 minute. Remove from heat. Add oats, nuts and vanilla. Mix well. Drop by heaping tablespoonfuls onto waxed paper. When cool, roll in a mixture of ground nuts, sugar and cinnamon. Store at room temperature or in the refrigerator. Keeps well for at least a week.

Rabbi Shimon Bar Yochai hid in a cave for 13 years because of the Roman government's edict against studying Torah. When he emerged from hiding, he was disturbed by seeing people involved only in working the land and in other physical needs while neglecting more spiritual matters and the study of Torah. When he saw a man carrying two sprigs of myrtle, he asked him why. The man replied, "One represents 'zachor' ('Remember the Sabbath') and one represents 'shamor' ('Guard the Sabbath'). When Rabbi Shimon bar Yohai heard this reply, he was set at ease knowing that people were using the physical world for spiritual goals.

(Talmud Bavli)

Sesame Seed Crunch

1 lb. (500 gm.) sesame seeds	1 Tbsp. oil
10 oz. (300 gm.) sugar	pinch of salt
2 Tbsp. oil	

Combine all ingredients except sesame seeds in pan. Bring to a boil over medium flame, stirring constantly. When boiling, add sesame seeds and continue to stir over low-medium flame until sesame seeds are lightly browned, about 15 minutes. Turn out mixture quickly, on a flat surface (tray, counter top, table) which has been dampened with water, roll out with a premoistened rolling pin and cut into desired shape. All this should be done quickly before mixture hardens.

Date Balls

Be on the lookout for recipes children can prepare independently. Encourage your child's independence and creativity while inculcating a love for Shabbos.

½ cup margarine	1 tsp. vanilla
¾ cup sugar	½ tsp. salt
½ lb. (400 gm.) dates, cut up	½ cup coconut
1 beaten egg	2 cups crisped rice
1 Tbsp. orange juice	

Place margarine, sugar and dates in a saucepan. Bring to boil and simmer until dates dissolve, stirring frequently. Combine egg, juice, vanilla and salt in another pot and cook for 2 minutes. Removes from heat and mix quickly into date mixture. Pour into a large bowl and stir in coconut and rice crisps. Refrigerate at least ½ hour to set. Form into balls.

Almond Brittle

2 cups sugar	1 cup coarsely chopped almonds

Melt sugar in a saucepan over a low to medium flame stirring with a wooden spoon to prevent burning. When sugar is completely melted and light brown in color, stir in almonds. Remove from flame and pour onto a marble slab or foil covered surface. Flatten immediately with back of spoon dipped in hot water.

Chocolate Nut Crunch

2 cups cookie crumbs
1 cup chopped walnuts
½ cup margarine
1 cup confectioner's sugar
3 egg yolks, beaten well

1½ oz. (45 gm.) melted parve
   chocolate
½ tsp. vanilla
3 egg whites, beaten stiff

Combine crumbs and nuts. Line bottom of 9-inch square pan with half of crumbs. Thoroughly cream margarine and sugar. Add beaten egg yolks, chocolate and vanilla. Mix well. Fold in beaten egg whites. Spread mixture over crumbs. Top with remaining crumbs. Refrigerate overnight. To serve, cut into squares.

Rum Balls

2 cups cake or cookie crumbs
½ cup sugar
2 Tbsp. cocoa
½ cup margarine

1 egg
2 Tbsp. rum or wine
coconut, chopped nuts or sprinkles

Mix together all ingredients except for last. Form into balls. Roll in coconut, chopped nuts or sprinkles and refrigerate. Serve at room temperature.
Variation: 1. Put a cherry or almond into center of each ball before rolling in coconut.   2. Add ½ cup chopped raisins or chopped nuts to mixture before forming balls.

Whoever sanctifies the Sabbath, whoever keeps the Sabbath from being profaned shall be greatly rewarded in accordance with his effort.

(Zemiroth)

Cakes, Cookies and Frostings

The unmistakable aroma of Shabbos baking heralds the end of the work week. Happy is the family whose leftover Shabbos cake can carry that special Shabbos flavor over to the beginning of the next week as well!

Cakes and cookies may be part of the meal menu, or they may be featured at a *kiddush* (or *shalom zachar*). They may also be prepared to have on hand for drop-in guests, or for Torah-learning sessions in the afternoon or even pre-dawn hours.

Baking Substitutions:

1 oz. semisweet chocolate =   3 Tbsp. cocoa plus
                                        1 Tbsp. shortening plus
                                        1 Tbsp. sugar

1 cup sugar = $7/8$ cup honey minus $1/4$ cup liquid
                                        per cup of honey

1 whole egg =   2 egg whites plus
                                        1 Tbsp. cornstarch or
                                        2 egg yolks

1 cup corn syrup =   1 cup sugar plus 1 cup water
                                        boiled down to 1 cup syrup.

1 cup white flour = $7/8$ cup whole wheat flour

1 cup sour milk =   1 Tbsp. vinegar plus
                                        1 Tbsp. oil plus
                                        water to 1 cup

Please note:

- Baking times may vary with altitude and weather conditions.
- Equivalencies have been approximated with common package sizes and weights and oven settings.
- Margarine means unsalted.
- The best way to check flour is to sift it, using a fine sifter.

Super Chiffon Cake

Infinitely variable; a different version can grace your table each week.

7 eggs, separated
1½ cups sugar
1 cup oil
1 tsp. vanilla
2 tsp. lemon juice

2¼ cups flour
pinch salt
3 tsp. baking powder
1 cup hot water

Separate eggs. Beat yolks with half the sugar, until thick. Add oil, vanilla, and lemon juice. Combine flour with salt and baking powder. Add dry ingredients alternately with hot water to yolk mixture, beating just until smooth. In a separate bowl, with clean beaters, beat egg whites, gradually adding remaining sugar until stiff. Gently fold the two mixtures together. Pour into ungreased tube pan. Bake at 350°F (175°C) for 40 minutes, until cake bounces back when lightly touched. Invert pan to cool.
Variations:
Lemon chiffon: Add 2 tsp. lemon extract. Use heated lemon juice instead of water, if desired. Frost with lemon frosting.
Coffee chiffon: Instead of water, use hot, strong coffee.
Almond-Marble swirl: Prepare basic batter and pour into pan all but ¼ cup. Combine ½ cup sugar, ½ cup cocoa, 2 Tbsp. warm water and 1 Tbsp. almond extract. Add this to the ¼ cup batter and swirl mixture through the white batter. When cake is cool, pour over it the following topping: 4 oz. (100 gm.) chocolate, 2 Tbsp. margarine and 2 tsp. brandy or wine, heated until combined.
Maple-Walnut Marble chiffon: Prepare basic batter. Pour all but one cup into pan. To the one cup, add 2 tsp. maple extract, 2 Tbsp. cocoa and ½ cup walnut pieces. Pour over batter in pan and fold in gently.

Chocolate Fudge Cake Without Eggs

3 cups flour
2 cups sugar
6 Tbsp cocoa
1 tsp. salt

2 tsp. vanilla   **2 cups warm water**
¾ cup oil
1 Tbsp. vinegar
2 tsp. baking soda

Sift dry ingredients together. Mix in vanilla, oil, vinegar and water. Beat until smooth. Bake in a 9 inch by 12 inch pan at 350° F (175° C) for 30-40 minutes. Frost with White Cream Icing, p. 113.

Eggs should be stored with the large end up. Cold eggs are easier to separate, but when egg whites are at room temperature they beat up to a larger volume. When beating egg whites, both bowl and beaters must be absolutely clean and dry. Even the smallest amount of yolk or oil in the egg whites or the bowl prevents good results. When beaten properly, egg whites should triple in volume.

102

Israeli Chocolate Cake With Instant Icing

2 oz (50 gm.) bittersweet chocolate   4 eggs, separated
4 Tbsp. cocoa   1 Tbsp. rum
½ cup water   2 Tbsp. wine
1½ cup sugar   1½ cups flour
1 cup margarine   3 tsp. baking powder

Heat chocolate, cocoa, water and sugar until sugar melts. Add margarine. Mix well. Cool in refrigerator. Add egg yolks, rum and wine. In a separate bowl, beat egg whites. Fold in flour and baking powder. Add to half of chocolate mixture, reserving remaining half for icing. Pour the cake mixture into an 8 inch by 8 inch pan and bake at 350° F (175° C) for 30 minutes. While cake is still warm, pour remaining chocolate mixture over it for instant icing.

When done, a cake shrinks slightly from the side of the pan and springs back when touched lightly. Or, test a cake to see if it is ready by inserting a wooden toothpick into the center of the cake. If it comes out clean, the cake is done.

Velvety Chocolate Cake

¾ cup margarine   1 cup warm mashed potatoes
1 cup sugar   2 cups flour
2 eggs   2 tsp. baking powder
½ cup water   ½ tsp. cinnamon
2 squares baking chocolate   ½ tsp. nutmeg
    or 2 oz. (50 gm.) bittersweet chocolate

Cream the margarine, add the sugar and eggs. Heat chocolate with water over low heat until chocolate melts. Cool slightly. Add with the mashed potatoes to margarine mixture and beat well. Gradually add dry ingredients. Bake at 350° F (175° C) in a 9 inch by 13 inch pan.

Hint: Instant mashed potatoes are perfect for this recipe.

Forgot to take out margarine from refrigerator? Soften it quickly by grating it into the bowl. Need eggs at room temperature quickly? Put them in a bowl of very hot tap water for 3-5 minutes.

103

Streusel Coffee Cake

¾ cup sugar
⅓ cup oil
1 egg
½ cup orange juice
 or any other juice
1½ cups flour
2 tsp. baking powder
¼ cup raisins (optional)

TOPPING:
½ cup brown sugar
2 Tbsp. flour
2 tsp. cinnamon
2 Tbsp. oil
½ cup finely chopped
 walnuts

Combine sugar, oil and egg. Add juice and beat thoroughly. Mix raisins with dry ingredients. Add flour/raisin mixture and beat until smooth. Spread in a greased 9″ square pan. Combine ingredients for topping with a fork and sprinkle over batter. Press down slightly. Bake at 375° F (185° C) for 30-35 minutes.

Before the Sabbath all kinds of tasty treats are prepared. While it is yet day, stuffed chickens are readied. Various delicacies and fragrant wines are arranged. We are bidden to enjoy fine foods at each of the three Sabbath meals.

(Zemiroth)

Easy Apple Coffee Cake

3 cups sliced apple
1 Tbsp. cinnamon
1½ cups + 4 Tbsp. sugar
3 cups flour
1 tsp. salt

3 tsp. baking powder
4 eggs
¼ cup orange juice
1 Tbsp. vanilla
1 cup oil

Toss sliced apples with cinnamon and 4 Tbsp. sugar in a bowl. Combine sifted dry ingredients in a large bowl. Make a well and add eggs, juice, vanilla and oil. Beat until smooth. In a lightly greased tube pan, spread ⅓ of dough. Drain off liquid from apples. Arrange half of them over dough. Cover with ⅓ dough. Spread rest of apples and cover with remainder of dough. Bake at 350° F (175° C) for 1-1¼ hours.

Sprinkle citrus or pineapple juice over fruit that may darken – apples, peaches, bananas, etc.

Fruit'n Nut Cake

3 cups flour	3 eggs
1 tsp. cinnamon	1 tsp. vanilla
1 tsp. baking soda	3 cups sliced apple
2 cups sugar	1 cup raisins
1 cup oil	1 cup walnut pieces

Combine ingredients in order listed. Spoon batter into a greased tube pan. Bake at 350° F (175° C) for 1-1¼ hours until done. Cake should bounce back when touched lightly.

Orange Carrot Cake

2 cups flour	1 tsp. salt
2 cups sugar	½ cup chopped nuts (optional)
2 tsp. baking powder	4 eggs
2 tsp. baking soda	¼ cup oil
2 tsp. cinnamon	2 cups grated carrots
2 tsp. nutmeg	1 large orange

Soak nuts overnight in salted water and nutmeats will come out whole when you crack them.

Mix dry ingredients and nuts. Add eggs and oil and mix well. Quarter orange. Do not peel. Remove pits. Blend orange in a blender. Add carrots and orange to flour mixture. Mix well. Bake at 350° F (175° C) in a tube pan or 2 loaf pans for 50-60 minutes.

Sifting flour is less messy if a large plastic bag is fastened round the sifter with a rubber band.

Old-Fashioned Honey Cake

2 eggs	1 tsp. cocoa
¾ cup honey	1 tsp. cinnamon
1 cup sugar	½ cup nuts
½ cup + 1 Tbsp. oil	2 cups sifted flour
1 tsp. baking soda	1 cup strong coffee
1 tsp. baking powder	

Combine eggs, honey, sugar and oil. Mix in dry ingredients alternating with liquid. Beat five minutes. Pour into 9" by 12" greased pan. Bake till done at 375°F (185° C).

A few drops of oil will prevent honey from sticking in the measuring cup, so measure oil first.

Honey Chiffon Cake

7 eggs, separated
¾ cup brown sugar
1 cup oil
1 cup hot coffee
2 tsp. wine
juice of half a lemon
6 Tbsp. honey

2¼ cups flour
¼ tsp. salt
2½ tsp. baking powder
1 tsp. soda
1 tsp. cinnamon
¾ cup white sugar

Beat egg yolks with brown sugar until thick. Add oil, beating slowly. Then add next nine ingredients in order, continuing to beat on a low mixer speed, until mixture is smooth. Beat whites with sugar in another bowl. Fold meringue into yolk mixture. Bake in an ungreased large tube pan at 350° F (175° C) for about 40 minutes or till cake bounces back when touched. Invert to cool. (If you don't have a large enough tube pan, pour some of the batter into cupcake tins. This cake rises high and will spill over. Do not fill any pan more than ⅔ full with this batter.)

Folding in egg whites properly is the secret to the lightness of chiffon or sponge cake. For best results, stir ¼ of the stiffly beaten egg whites into the batter. Pile the rest of the egg whites on top of the batter and fold in carefully and thoroughly with a rubber spatula.

Shabbos Strudel

DOUGH:
2½ cups flour
½ tsp. baking powder
⅛ tsp. salt
2 small or 1 large egg
5 Tbsp. oil
1 cup cold orange juice

FILLING:
6 cups peeled and chopped apples

1 lemon, grated rind, pulp and
   juice, without pits
6 Tbsp. sugar
½ tsp. nutmeg
½ cup raisins
1 cup chopped almonds
6 Tbsp. coconut (optional)
1 cup bread crumbs
½ cup oil
powdered sugar

Dough: Mix dry ingredients of dough recipe. Beat eggs and mix in oil and juice. Slowly add dry ingredients until dough is solid enough to handle. Place dough on a well floured board and cover with a bowl. Let rest for ½ hour while preparing filling.

Filling: Mix together first 6 or 7 ingredients of filling and set aside. Roll dough out, as thinly as possible without tearing a hole. Oil the dough and spread ½ of bread crumbs on it, reserving some oil to brush on top. Put on apple filling and sprinkle remaining crumbs. With both hands, carefully roll up the strudel. Seal ends. Brush top of strudel with oil. Bake at 375° F (185° C) for 50 minutes until brown. Cut into 2-inch slices. Sprinkle with powdered sugar. Serves 12.

Add raisins to flour before mixing them into the batter and the raisins won't all sink to the bottom of the cake.

Triple Decker Jam Cake

1 cup margarine
1¾ cup + 3 Tbsp. sugar
4 eggs, separated
¼ cup orange or lemon juice
3 cups flour
3 tsp. baking powder
grated lemon peel (optional)

3 Tbsp. cocoa
3 Tbsp. jam
3 Tbsp. water
3 tsp. vanilla sugar
    or 1 tsp. vanilla extract
½ cup chopped nuts (optional)

Cream margarine with ¾ cup sugar. Add egg yolks and juice. Mix well. Add flour, baking powder and lemon peel and knead until dough is smooth. Spread half of dough into a 9 inch by 13 inch pan. Add cocoa and 3 Tbsp. sugar to remaining dough. Spread this dough on top of first layer in pan. Bake at 350° F (175° C) for 30 minutes (until dough is firm but not dry). Mix jam and water together and spread over cake. Beat egg whites. Add 1 cup sugar and vanilla. Spread over jam layer. Sprinkle nuts over meringue. Bake an additional 10 minutes, until meringue is lightly browned.

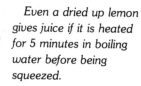

Even a dried up lemon gives juice if it is heated for 5 minutes in boiling water before being squeezed.

Linzertorte

2 cups flour
1½ cups finely ground nuts
¾ cup sugar
¾ cup margarine
2 eggs
2 tsp. grated lemon peel

¼ tsp. salt
¼ tsp. cinnamon
⅛ tsp. ground cloves
1½ cups raspberry jam
2 tsp. lemon juice
1 egg, beaten

Measure first 9 ingredients into bowl. Combine with fork or mixer at low speed until blended and then mix well. Form ball, wrap in waxed paper and refrigerate 3 hours or till firm. Preheat oven to 350° F (175° C). Press about ¾ of dough on bottom and 1 inch up sides of greased 9-inch springform pan. Combine jam and lemon juice. Spread over crust. Then, on floured surface, roll out remaining dough about ¼ inch thick. Cut into 8 ¾-inch strips. Make lattice top. Brush strips with beaten egg. Bake 50 minutes, till golden brown. Makes 16 servings.

Clean darkened aluminum pans by filling them with a mixture of 2 teaspoons cream of tartar in a quart of water. Boil for 10 minutes.

Jelly Roll Cake

1 cup flour
1 tsp. baking powder
¼ tsp. salt
1 tsp. vanilla
4 eggs, separated
¾ cup sugar

¼ cup orange juice or water
confectioner's sugar

FILLING:
jelly, ice cream or chocolate
    cream filling

Sift flour, baking powder and salt together. Beat egg yolks with ½ cup sugar. Add vanilla. Add flour mixture and juice alternately while mixing well slowly. Beat egg whites until stiff with remaining ¼ cup sugar. Fold in egg white mixture. Line a greased sheet cake pan, 10 inch by 15 inch with greased wax paper. Pour batter in. Spread cake evenly. Bake at 350° F (175° C) for 15-20 minutes, until lightly browned. Invert cake pan onto towel sprinkled with confectioner's sugar. Slowly peel off wax paper while loosely rolling towel. Let rolled cake cool. Open. Spread with jelly, chocolate cream filling, or ice cream and reroll.
Variation: Substitute ¼ cup cocoa for ½ cup flour and increase sugar by ¼ cup for chocolate roll.

Chocolate Cream Filling

¾ cup sugar
1 cup soft margarine
1 Tbsp. water
2 Tbsp. wine

1 tsp. vanilla
2 eggs
2 tsp. instant coffee
1 Tbsp. cocoa

Pulverize sugar in blender, or use confectioner's sugar. Gradually add all ingredients. Blend until smooth. Spread filling on cooled cake and roll again. Spread some filling on outside and garnish with chopped nuts or coconut. Freeze. Defrost only slightly before serving.

Why do we ask of G-d each and every Sabbath, "Please bequeath to us your holy Sabbath?" After all, the Jewish nation long ago received the gift of Sabbath.

Nevertheless, each Sabbath that arrives is a fresh gift. And so we ask each week that the gift of the current Sabbath be bestowed upon us.

(*Sefas Emes*)

Since baked goods freeze well, it's a good idea to bake a double recipe and freeze half each time you bake. Then, during a busy week you can skip baking and defrost instead. Or, you can serve up a varied platter of cakes without baking several each week.

Spice Loaf

2 cups flour
1 tsp. cinnamon
1 tsp. cloves
½ tsp. allspice
½ tsp. salt
1 tsp. baking soda
2 tsp. baking powder

2 eggs
2 cups brown sugar, or
   1 cup sugar + 2 Tbsp. molasses
1 cup water
1 Tbsp. vinegar
⅔ cup oil

Sift all dry ingredients together. Beat eggs until thick and lemon colored. Beat in sugar, add water and vinegar alternately with the dry ingredients, combining well. Stir in oil. Pour into greased or foil-lined loaf pan. Bake at 375° F (185° C) for at least 40 minutes.

Chocolate Date Cake

1¾ cups flour
1 cup sugar
2 eggs
¾ cup margarine
¾ tsp. baking powder
½ tsp. salt

4 oz. (100 gm.) chocolate, melted
   and cooled
1 cup pitted dates
1½ tsp. baking soda
1½ cups boiling water

Keep dates and raisins fresh by storing in a tightly covered jar with a piece of citrus rind. Chop them easily with a lightly greased knife.

Mix flour, sugar, eggs, margarine, baking powder, salt and chocolate. Blend dates, baking soda and water. Add to flour mixture. Bake at 350° F (175° C) for 45 minutes in a 9 inch by 12 inch pan.

Best Brownies

1 cup margarine
2 cups brown sugar
½ cup cocoa, or 4 oz. (100 gm.)
   bittersweet chocolate, melted
4 eggs

pinch of salt
2 tsp. vanilla
1 cup flour
1 cup chopped nuts

Cream margarine with sugar. Add cocoa or chocolate and mix well. Add eggs, salt, vanilla, flour and nuts. Bake in a 9 inch by 13 inch greased pan at 350°F (175° C) for 30 minutes.
Note: White sugar may be substituted for brown.

Brownies are chewier after being frozen and defrosted.

109

Yeast Cake Dough

2 oz. (60 gm.) yeast	2 eggs
2 cups boiling water + ½ cup	1 cup + 1 Tbsp. sugar
lukewarm water	rind of ½ lemon, grated
1 cup margarine	7-8 cups flour

Dissolve yeast in lukewarm water and add 1 Tbsp. sugar. Cover and let stand 5-10 minutes, until foamy. Place margarine in large mixing bowl. Pour boiling water over margarine to melt it. Let stand. When cooled, add yeast mixture, eggs, sugar, lemon rind. Slowly add flour, a few cups at a time. When all the flour has been added, knead dough very well for about 5 minutes on a floured surface. Add a bit more flour if too sticky. It may be put into a electric mixer or kneaded by hand. Dust dough with flour. Cover with a towel and let rise in a warm place for 3-4 hours, or overnight in the refrigerator. Divide dough into 6 balls. Roll out dough and fill with any of the listed fillings.

Braided Yeast Cake

Fill and roll basic yeast dough as desired. With sharp knife or scissors, cut lengthwise through center of roll nearly to end. Twist one half over other to the end of the roll. Fasten ends together. The visible filling adds appeal.

FILLINGS:

Chocolate Yeast Cake

½ cup cocoa	1 egg, separated
1 cup sugar	¼ cup bread crumbs
¼ cup water	melted margarine or oil

Roll basic yeast dough into rectangles. Spread with melted margarine or oil. Mix rest of ingredients together, except for egg yolk, and spread on dough. Roll up in jelly roll fashion. Place in pan. Let rise again 30-60 minutes. Brush on egg yolk. Bake at 350° F (175° C) for 45 minutes. Fills 3 rolls.

Yeast needs warm water to grow. Hot water can kill it.

Active yeast dissolves and grows in about 10 minutes. Test it – if it is not active, don't use it.

Yeast dough rises better if placed in a pan where it touches the sides. This will force dough to expand upward.

Cinnamon Sugar Yeast Cake

½ cup sugar
1 tsp. cinnamon
1 egg yolk

1 tsp. water
chopped nuts or raisins (optional)
melted margarine or oil

Brush oil or melted margarine over rolled out dough. Sprinkle with sugar and cinnamon. Add chopped nuts or raisins for extra flavor. Roll up. Brush with egg yolk mixed with water, if desired. Let rise and bake at 350° F (175° C) for 45 minutes.

Apple Filled Yeast Cake

3 large tart apples
½ cup raisins
½ cup sugar

2 tsp. cinnamon
½ cup chopped nuts
1 Tbsp. lemon juice

Slice apples thinly. Combine all ingredients. Spread on rolled out dough. Roll up. Let rise and bake at 350° F (175° C) for 45 minutes.

Creamy White Cake

1 cup margarine
2 cups sugar
3 eggs
1 tsp. vanilla

1 tsp. salt
2 tsp. baking powder
3 cups flour
1 cup juice

Cream together margarine and sugar. Mix in eggs, vanilla, salt and baking powder. Add flour and juice alternately. Bake at 350° F (175° C) for 40 minutes in a 9 inch by 12 inch pan. Cover with chocolate frosting.

Chocolate Frosting

½ tsp. vanilla
4 Tbsp. cocoa
4 Tbsp. oil

⅓ tsp. coffee
4 Tbsp. hot water
2 cups confectioner's sugar

Mix together all ingredients. Spread on cooled cake.

Raisins and dried fruit are tastier and juicier if soaked in warm water before adding to dough.

To split a cake into layers, insert toothpicks all around at halfway mark. Rest the blade of the knife on the toothpicks and cut towards the center. Continue all around the cake. Then cut right through.

Macaroon Cake

6 eggs, separated	3 cups flour
1½ cups margarine	1 cup water
3 cups sugar	2 cups shredded coconut
½ tsp. each almond and coconut	
or 1 tsp. almond extract	

Beat egg yolks, margarine and 2 cups sugar, till thick and creamy. Add flavoring, then stir in flour alternately with water. Add shredded coconut. Beat egg whites with remaining sugar until stiff. Fold in and bake at 300° F (150° C) for 1¼ hours in a 9 inch by 13 inch pan, or up to 2 hours in a tube pan. This is a pound cake with a surprising twist.

Apple Muffins

1 egg	½ tsp. salt
½ cup water or juice	½ cup raisins (optional)
¼ cup oil	
1 cup chopped apple	
1½ cups flour	TOPPING:
½ cup sugar	1 tsp. cinnamon
2 tsp. baking powder	¼ cup brown sugar
	¼ cup chopped nuts (optional)

Combine ingredients for batter in order listed and mix until smooth. Pour into 12-muffin tin. Mix topping ingredients together and sprinkle over each muffin. Bake at 400° F (200° C) for 20 minutes.
Variation: Substitute ¾ cup whole wheat flour for half of the flour quantity. Reduce sugar to ¼ cup.

When I was about nine years old, my father and my uncle used to rise at midnight on Friday night and learn together until it was time for the morning prayers. I too, would learn part of the night with them, and my righteous mother got up and learned Midrash and the weekly portion with the commentaries of the Malbim and the Ramban. When she joined us, I felt the festiveness of the occasion. She would serve us hot coffee and special oven baked cakes, which were wondrously delicious. To be sure, the prime purpose of our early rising was to learn Torah, yet I cannot deny that those cakes played an important part in my eagerness to jump out of bed!

(Michtav Me'Eliyahu)

FROSTINGS

Professional Fluff Icing

1½ cups sugar
½ cup water
1 Tbsp. honey or corn syrup
½ tsp. salt

2 egg whites
1 tsp. vanilla
food coloring, optional

Combine sugar, water, honey and salt in saucepan. Heat gradually till sugar dissolves, about 5 minutes. Remove from heat. In clean mixing bowl, beat whites stiff. Continue beating while gradually adding hot sugar syrup and vanilla. Beat 5 minutes more, or until very thick. Add coloring if desired. Spread sides and then top of cake.

Confectioner's sugar frosting won't crack if you add a pinch of baking powder while mixing it.

Creamy White Frosting

1 cup margarine
1 lb. (400 gm.) confectioner's sugar
2 Tbsp. cornstarch
¼ cup egg whites (about 2)

¼ tsp. salt
½ tsp. vanilla
¼ tsp. almond extract

Beat all ingredients together in mixer. Frost cooled cake with frosting. Color with food coloring if desired.
Variation: Use different flavorings.

White Cream Icing

½ cup sugar
¼ cup water

½ cup margarine
1 tsp. vanilla

Melt sugar and water together over low flame. Cool completely. Whip margarine and vanilla while adding sugar syrup. Spread over cooled cake.

For crumbless icing: Brush crumbs off cake with pastry brush. Frost twice, first a thin coat then frost again.

Easy Chocolate Glaze

6 oz. (150 gm.) chocolate
5 Tbsp. water

3 Tbsp. sugar
⅓ cup margarine

Melt all ingredients in a double boiler. Mix and spread,while hot onto a cooled cake.

Israeli Chocolate Cream Frosting

For perfect frosting, never frost a cake until it is completely cool.

⅛ cup water
4 Tbsp. cocoa
½-¾ cup sugar

½ cup margarine
1 tsp. vanilla

Boil water, cocoa and sugar together until thick. Cool slightly. Add margarine and vanilla. Cream together. Spread over cake or use as a filling.

Creamy Chocolate Frosting

1¾ cups margarine
1 lb. (400 gm.) confectioner's sugar
¾ cup cocoa
3 egg yolks

3 tsp. vanilla
5 tsp. instant coffee, dissolved in
   5 Tbsp. boiling water

Combine ingredients in order listed in mixing bowl. Beat at high speed until light and fluffy (about 5-10 minutes). Spread over cake. Enough for 2 tube cakes.

Coffee Cream Icing

The custom of singing zemiroth is mentioned in the Talmud. Rava said: "On the Sabbath, the Jewish people eat, drink, discuss Torah and sing praises."

1 cup margarine
1 cup brown sugar
2 egg yolks

2 tsp. instant coffee, dissolved
   in 2 Tbsp. boiling water
1 Tbsp. cornstarch

Combine ingredients in blender jar, blending until smooth. Transfer to mixer bowl, and whip till fluffy.

114

COOKIES & PASTRY

Spumoni Cookies

1 cup margarine
1½ cups confectioner's sugar
1 tsp. vanilla
1 egg
2½ cups flour

1 Tbsp. cocoa
½ tsp. rum flavoring
½ tsp. almond flavoring
red and green food coloring
½ cup nuts, chopped

Combine first 5 ingredients to form dough. Divide this dough into 3 equal parts. To first third, add cocoa. To second third, add rum flavoring and a few drops of red food coloring. To last part, add almond flavoring, a few drops of green food coloring and nuts. Form a long flat rectangle out of each third, patting smooth. Pile them one on top of the other, with the green in the middle, making a 3 color log. Freeze for at least an hour or for as long as you like until ready to bake. Slice thin and bake on ungreased cookie sheet about 8 minutes at 375° F (180° C) until firm. Do not allow cookies to brown or they will lose their pretty colors.

Honey Drops

1 cup margarine
1 cup brown sugar
2 eggs
6 Tbsp. honey

1 tsp. vanilla
3½ cups sifted flour
2 tsp. baking soda

Combine ingredients in order listed. Chill dough until firm, preferably in freezer. Pull off small pieces and roll into balls of approximately 1 inch (2.5 cm.) diameter. Place on ungreased cookie sheet and flatten with heel of hand. Bake at 350° F (175° C) for 10-12 minutes. Delicious individually or sandwiched together with jam.

Meringue Drops

3 egg whites
¾ cup sugar
½ tsp. vanilla

½ cup grated chocolate,
    chopped dates or coconut

Beat egg whites until frothy. Gradually add sugar and vanilla. Beat until stiff. Fold in chocolate, dates or coconut. Drop by tablespoonfuls onto a greased cookie sheet. Bake in a slow oven, 250° F (125° C) until dry, about 50-60 minutes.

How to keep your energetic children constructively entertained during an elegant four course dinner? Prepare an activity along with the courses. Draw up a quiz on the weekly portion or on an upcoming holiday. The questions should be geared to the different levels of the children so that all will enjoy and learn from the competition.

115

Chocolate Chip Cookies

1 cup margarine	2¼ cups flour
¾ cup white sugar	1 tsp. baking powder
¾ cup brown sugar	1 tsp. salt
1 tsp. vanilla	2 cups chocolate bits
2 eggs	

Cream together margarine, sugar and vanilla. Mix in eggs. Add remaining ingredients and mix well. Drop onto a greased cookie sheet by spoonfuls. Bake at 350° F (175° C) for 8-10 minutes.

Peanut Butter Chocolate Bars

½ cup margarine	8 oz. (200 gm.) bittersweet chocolate
½ cup brown sugar	2 Tbsp. corn syrup
1¼ cups flour	2 Tbsp. water
½ tsp. salt	½ cup chopped nuts
peanut butter	

Combine margarine, brown sugar, flour and salt. Press onto bottom of 9 inch by 13 inch pan. Bake at 350° F (175° C) for 20 minutes, until golden brown (but not hard). Immediately spread peanut butter over this crust. Melt chocolate with remaining ingredients in a saucepan and pour over peanut butter. Sprinkle top with chopped nuts.

Jam-Filled Bars

1¼ cups margarine	1 cup chopped nuts
1 cup brown sugar	1½ cups jam
3 cups flour	1-2 tsp. lemon juice
1 tsp. baking soda	⅓ cup oatmeal

Combine first 5 ingredient sinto a crumbly dough. Press two-thirds into a 9 inch by 12 inch pan. Bake at 400° F (200° C) for 12 minutes. Combine jam with lemon juice and spread over dough. Sprinkle oatmeal over jam. Crumble remaining dough mixture over oatmeal layer. Bake 25 more minutes. Cut while hot, but leave in pan till cold.

Once a Jew who owned a cow for ploughing his fields became poor and sold his animal to a non-Jew. For six days the cow ploughed his new master's field, but on the seventh day it lay down under the yoke. Despite the blows of its new master, the cow wouldn't budge. When the master saw this he went to the Jew from whom he had bought the cow. "Come take back your cow. As much as I hit it, it won't move from its place." Understanding that the cow was used to resting on the Sabbath, the Jew replied, "I'll make it work".

Approaching the cow, the original master said, "Dear cow, you know that as long as I owned you, you worked six days and rested on the Sabbath. Now, my sins have

Oatmeal Cookies

1 cup margarine
1¼ cups brown sugar
2 eggs
1½ tsp. vanilla
1 tsp. salt

1 tsp. cinnamon
1 tsp. baking soda
2 cups oatmeal
2 cups flour
⅓ cup water

Cream margarine with sugar. Mix in eggs. Mix in remaining ingredients. Drop by spoonfuls onto cookie sheet. Bake for 15 minutes at 350° F (175° C).
Variation: Add ½ cup raisins or ½ cup chopped nuts or ½ cup chocolate chips.

Velvet Cookies

1 cup shortening
2 Tbsp. peanut butter
1 cup confectioner's sugar
1 egg
1 tsp. vanilla

½ tsp. almond extract
2 cups sifted flour
½ tsp. baking powder
¼ tsp. salt

Combine all ingredients in order listed to form thick dough. When dough is ready, it may be refrigerated, frozen or used right away. It may be forced through a cookie press or shaped into balls and flattened on a cookie sheet. Bake at 400° F (200° C) for 8-10 minutes. Makes about 50 cookies.

"Mandel" Brodt

¾ cup margarine
1 cup sugar
1 tsp. vanilla
3 eggs

3 cups flour
1 tsp. baking powder
¾ cup chopped walnuts
1 tsp. cinnamon (optional)

Mix all ingredients in order listed to form a thick dough. Divide dough in half and shape into 2 loaves on a greased cookie sheet. Bake at 350° F (175° C) for 30 minutes. Slice into ½-inch (1.5 cm.) slices. Lay slices on side in another pan and bake 5-10 minutes more.
Variation: Divide dough in half. Add 3 Tbsp. cocoa, 4 Tbsp. sugar, 1 Tbsp. oil to 1 half. Shape the white and chocolate parts into 2 loaves each. Slit each white loaf down the middle and "hide" a chocolate loaf inside each. Bake as above.

reduced me to poverty and I was compelled to sell you to a non-Jew. So please, stand up and plough the field." Immediately, the cow stood on its feet and began to work.

The new owner was astonished. He insisted that the Jew reveal the secret whispered into the cow's ear. When the original owner repeated what he had told the cow, the non-Jew began to tremble. He said, "If a cow without speech and understanding recognizes its Creator, I, who was created in His image and given understanding, shall I not recognize my Creator?" He proceeded to convert to Judaism and began to study Torah. Rabbi Yohanan ben Toratha ("toratha" means cow in Aramaic) became such a great scholar that even today we study laws that he taught.

(*Pesikta Rabasi*)

Elegant Lace Cookies

1 cup margarine, melted	⅔ cup flour
2 cups oatmeal (uncooked)	¼ cup water
1 cup sugar	½ tsp. salt

Stir all ingredients together. Drop by scant teaspoonfuls, at least 2-inches apart on a cookie sheet. These cookies spread out and become very thin. Bake at 325° F (160° C) for 10-12 minutes, or until golden. Lift with metal spatula and lay over rolling pin to give a curved shape. Cool. If cookies harden before shaping, put in oven for 2 minutes to soften.

Shabbos is not only the best time to teach our children through study. It is also the ideal day to train our children in the performance of mitzvot that their busy schedules don't allow them time for during the week.

Visiting the sick and elderly is a mitzvah that is especially appropriate for Shabbos. Shabbos itself is endowed with a special healing power so that visits are doubly worthwhile on this day.

Rich No-Knead Rogelach

1 oz. (30 gm.) fresh yeast	1 cup margarine
or 1 package instant dried yeast	1 tsp. salt
½ cup + 2 Tbsp. sugar	2 eggs, separated
¼ cup warm water	1 tsp. cinnamon
2 cups flour	1 cup chopped nuts

Dissolve yeast and 2 Tbsp. sugar in warm water. Set aside. Mix flour, margarine and salt with a fork until evenly crumbly. Add beaten egg yolks and yeast mixture to dough. Mix well. Divide dough into fourths. Roll each fourth into a circle about 8 to 12 inches (20-30 cm.) in diameter. Beat egg whites with ½ cup sugar and cinnamon. Spread some of this meringue onto each circle, almost up to the perimeter. Sprinkle with nuts. Cut each circle into 12 wedges. Roll each up from widest part to narrowest. Bake on cookie sheets at 350° F (175° C) for 8-10 minutes.

Rogelach

Flaky Pastry Dough (see	2 tsp. cinnamon
next recipe)	melted margarine or oil
1 cup sugar	½ cup chopped nuts (optional)

Divide dough into eighths. Form balls. Roll each ball into a 7-inch circle. Brush with melted margarine. Sprinkle with sugar, nuts and cinnamon. Cut into eighths as for a pie. Roll each wedge from outside edge towards center. Bake on baking sheet at 425° F (200° C) for 15 minutes, then 375° F (185° C) for 10-15 minutes.

Flaky Pastry Dough

(This is a basic dough to use for rogelach, knishes, etc.)

2 cups flour
½ tsp. salt
¾ cup margarine

⅓ cup cold water
1 egg yolk
2 Tbsp. vinegar

Sift flour and salt together. Cut in margarine with a pastry cutter or 2 knives until dough resembles peas. In a separate cup, mix together cold water, egg yolk and vinegar. Sprinkle a little at a time into flour/margarine mixture. Work with fingers or with fork only until thoroughly combined. Add water, if necessary. Dough should not be sticky. You may require 1 or 2 tablespoons more water depending on type of flour and temperature. Shape dough into ball. Place in plastic bag and refrigerate for at least 2 hours. This dough will keep refrigerated for several days and can be frozen as well. Roll out on slightly floured surface. Do not handle more than necessary.

Variation: Egg yolk can be eliminated if water is increased to ½ cup.

The consistency of dough varies with various flours and weather conditions, so don't hesitate to adjust flour and liquid as necessary. See p. 2 for halachah *concerning "separating challah"*

Apple Pie

Pastry for 2-crust pie (see "Lemon Meringue Pie" p. 120, or use prepared crust)
10 tart medium-sized apples
⅔ cup sugar (brown or white)
1 tsp. oil

2 Tbsp. flour
1 tsp. cinnamon
½ tsp. nutmeg
(1 tsp. lemon juice, if apples are not tart)

Roll out bottom crust, and fit into 9-inch pan. Peel and slice apples and pile them into the crust. Pour the sugar evenly over the apples. Drizzle the oil and sprinkle the flour and spices. Toss gently without damaging crust. Roll out pastry for top crust and cover the filling. Pinch crusts together and make three slits in the center. Bake in a hot oven 400° F (200° C) for 40 minutes or so, till crust is light brown.

Variation: Substitute 6 cups thinly sliced peaches or other fruit for apples.

"When the Sabbath comes, contentment comes."

(Talmud Bavli)

Lemon Meringue Pie

CRUST:

¾ cup margarine

¾-1 cup sugar

2 eggs

2 Tbsp. juice

2 cups flour

2 tsp. baking powder

½ tsp. salt

1 tsp. vanilla

Cream sugar and margarine for 2 minutes. Mix in eggs. Add remaining ingredients. Mix well until it becomes a soft dough. Refrigerate for 1 hour to make handling easier. This dough can be frozen, raw or baked. It is sufficient for 2 pie shells. Roll out in a circle. Line pie dish and bake at 350° F (175° C) for 20-30 minutes.

FILLING:

1½ cups sugar

⅓ cup flour

⅓ cup cornstarch

½ tsp. salt

2 Tbsp. margarine

2 cups boiling water

4 eggs, separated

½ cup lemon juice

1 Tbsp. lemon rind

2 Tbsp. sugar

Combine dry ingredients in a heavy saucepan. Add boiling water slowly, stirring with a wooden spoon until smooth. Cook over medium heat until mixture thickens and boils, stirring constantly. Remove ½ cup of hot mixture to small bowl. Add egg yolks, lemon juice and rind and mix together. Quickly pour back into pot. Reduce heat to low and cook, stirring slowly, 2 more minutes. Add margarine. Remove from heat. While hot, pour into baked shell. Cool. Beat whites with 2 Tbsp. sugar till stiff. Pile onto cooled filling. Bake for 15 minutes at 400° F (200° C). Cool away from draft.

Choosing citrus fruit? Pick fruit that is heavy for its size. Smoother, thinner skin indicates more juice.

And the children of Israel shall keep the Sabbath, to observe the Sabbath throughout their generations, as an eternal covenant. It is a sign between Me and the children of Israel forever, for in six days the L-rd made heaven and earth and on the seventh day He rested and was refreshed.

(Exodus 31)

120

WHOLE WHEAT FLOUR RECIPES

Country Raisin Cake

1 cup brown sugar
⅔ cup oil
2 cups raisins
1 cup water
¼ tsp. cloves
½ tsp. nutmeg

½ tsp. cinnamon
¼ tsp. allspice
2 cups whole wheat flour
1 tsp. baking powder
½ tsp. baking soda
¾ cup chopped nuts (optional)

Boil first 8 ingredients together for 4 minutes. Cool and add remaining ingredients. Bake in greased 9-inch square pan at 350° F (175° C) for 35 minutes.
Variation: Add half a banana, mashed, to batter.

Zucchini Cake

2½ cups whole wheat flour
½ cup wheat germ
1 tsp. baking soda
½ tsp. baking powder
2 cups sugar
3 tsp. cinnamon

½ tsp. nutmeg
1 cup oil
3 eggs, beaten
2 cups (about 3 medium) zucchini, grated
1 cup chopped nuts (optional)

Combine dry ingredients. Add remaining ingredients. Bake at 350° F (175° C) for about 1 hour in a 9 inch by 12 inch pan.

Pumpkin Cake

1½ cups sugar
1 cup oil
2 cups cooked pumpkin, drained
4 eggs, lightly beaten
3 cups whole wheat flour
2 Tbsp. cinnamon

2 tsp. baking powder
1 tsp. baking soda
2 tsp. vanilla
1 cup chopped nuts (optional)
1 cup raisins

Mix all ingredients together in a large bowl. Bake in tube pan at 350° F (175° C) for about 1 hour.

And it shall come to pass if you diligently hearken to me, said the L-rd, to bring no burden through the gates of this city on the Sabbath day and sanctify the Sabbath day doing no work on it. Then kings and princes sitting on the throne of David, riding chariots and horses, shall enter the gates of this city, they and their princes, the men of Judah, and the inhabitants of Jerusalem, and this city shall remain forever.

(Jeremiah 17)

Applesauce Oatmeal Cake

1¼ cups applesauce (sweetened)	1 egg
¾ cup oatmeal	1¼ cups whole wheat flour
1 cup raisins	1 tsp. baking soda
½ cup margarine	1 tsp. cinnamon
¾ cup sugar	¼ tsp. ground cloves

Heat applesauce, oats and raisins just below boiling and set aside for 20 minutes. Preheat oven to 350° F (175° C). Cream margarine and sugar until light and fluffy. Beat in egg. Stir dry ingredients into creamed mixture alternately with applesauce mixture. Pour into greased 9-inch square pan and bake 50-55 minutes, or until done. Canned applesauce may be used, but homemade will make this recipe extra special.

Oatmeal Cake

1¼ cups boiling water	1 tsp. vanilla
1 cup rolled oats	1½ cups whole wheat flour
½ cup margarine	1 tsp. baking powder
1 cup brown sugar, packed	½ tsp. baking soda
½ cup honey	1 tsp. cinnamon
2 eggs	

Pour boiling water over oats. Set aside to cool. Mix margarine, brown sugar, honey, eggs and vanilla. Add whole wheat flour, baking powder, baking soda and cinnamon alternately with oats/water mixture. Pour into greased 9-inch square pan. Bake at 350° F (175° C) for 45 minutes. May be baked in a 9 inch by 13 inch pan for a flatter cake.

Crunchy Oatmeal Cake

(Tastes like an oatmeal cookie; bakes like a cake)

2 cups oatmeal	2 tsp. baking powder
1 cup whole wheat flour	¾ cup brown sugar
½ cup oil	½ cup coconut, nuts, raisins or
2 eggs	wheat germ (optional)

Mix oil with sugar. Add eggs, beat well. Stir oats, flour, baking powder together and add to mixture. Press into greased pan and bake at 350° F (175° C) until firm. *Variation:* Spread half the batter into pan. Top with chopped dates or sliced apples sprinkled with cinnamon. Spread over remaining batter and bake.

Sesame Seed Cookies

1 cup sesame seeds	1 tsp. vanilla
¾ cup margarine	2 cups whole wheat flour
1 cup brown sugar	1 tsp. baking powder
2 eggs	½ tsp. baking soda
1 Tbsp. water	½ cup coconut

Lightly toast sesame seed in an ungreased skillet over a medium flame for 2-3 minutes. Beat together margarine, sugar, egg and vanilla. Add dry ingredients. Mix well. Form into balls and place on ungreased cookie sheet. Flatten with a fork. Bake at 350° F (175° C) for 10-12 minutes, or as bars for 20-25 minutes.

The Holy One, Blessed be He, said to Moses: I have (in my treasure house) a special gift, called the Sabbath, and I wish to give it to the people of Israel. Go and tell them!
(Talmud Bavli)

SHALOSH SEUDOTH

The third Sabbath meal customarily is referred to as *shalosh seudoth* — literally, "three meals." The name highlights its special importance. The Sabbath commandments include the eating of three meals. But the evening and morning meals are timed so that we would eat and enjoy them even without being commanded to do so. When we sit down, late in the afternoon, to this third meal, we do so only because the Sabbath requires it, not necessarily because we are hungry. This meal, then, is eaten only because of the *mitzvah* of *shalosh seudoth*. By eating it, we prove that we would have likewise eaten the other two meals, even had we not been hungry, thus demonstrating their *mitzvah* character as well. It is by eating this third meal, then, that we merit the reward for eating all three meals.

For this reason, although meat and chicken are not usually served at this meal, the homemaker tries to prepare some special dish in honor of *shalosh seudoth*.

Recipes from the salad, kugel, and various dessert sections may be suitable for this meal in addition to those in this section.

Salade Niçoise

	DRESSING:
1 can solid white tuna, flaked	½ cup oil
1 cup cooked potatoes, cubed	⅓ cup vinegar
1 cup cooked string beans	½ tsp. salt
1 can sprats, or sardines, drained	½ tsp. sugar
3 hard-boiled eggs, halved	2 cloves garlic, crushed
or quartered	¼ tsp. pepper
2-3 firm tomatoes, cut in wedges	
12 pitted black olives	
3 thin slices of onion	

Attractively arrange all ingredients, except onion rings, in serving bowl. (Each could be one wedge in a round bowl). Top with onion rings. Pour dressing over all. Refrigerate till serving time. Bring to the table *before* tossing to combine. Serves 8.

Vegetable Fish Cakes

1 lb. (½ kg.) cooked or	5 eggs
canned fish	½-¾ cup bread crumbs, matzah
2 medium potatoes	meal or oatmeal
2 small carrots	½ tsp. salt (or more to taste)
1 onion	oil for frying

Mash the fish. Combine potatoes, carrots, onion and eggs in blender or food processor until vegetables are finely ground. Add to fish. Add bread crumbs or other thickening, till liquid is absorbed and mixture is not too thin. Add salt and any other seasoning desired. Heat oil and fry by spoonfuls. Refrigerate fish cakes. Serve cold with sauce.

Fish sauce: Combine equal amounts of ketchup and prepared red horseradish.

Tartar sauce: Chop 3 small sour pickles fine. Stir ¾ cup mayonnaise into chopped pickles.

Pickled Fish

2 lb. (1 kg.) mackerel or grey mullet
coarse salt
3 sliced onions
¼ cup sugar
1 cup vinegar

1 cup water
1 lemon
2 bay leaves
3-4 cloves

Clean fish. Slice into 1-inch (2.5 cm.) slices. Sprinkle salt liberally over each piece. Refrigerate at least 2 hours. Prepare sauce by cooking 1 onion in water to cover for 10 minutes. Add sugar, vinegar and water and boil 10 minutes longer. Taste and adjust seasonings. Add fish slices and simmer for 20 minutes. Peel lemon and slice thin. Add lemon slices, bay leaves and cloves and cook another 5 minutes. Remove lemon slices and spices. Cool. Remove fish pieces and onions and transfer to a deep container. Add the other 2 sliced onions. Strain remaining soup over fish and onions. This can keep in the refrigerator for 1-2 weeks.

Gourmet Fillets in Wine Sauce

2 cups sliced onion
¼ cup oil
¼ cup raisins
2 Tbsp. slivered almonds (optional)
1 tsp. salt

⅛ tsp. pepper
1 Tbsp. honey or sugar
½ cup white wine
¼ cup vinegar
1½ lbs. (700 gm.) fish fillets

Sauté onion in oil on a low flame until tender, but not brown. Remove onions to a plate. Add rest of ingredients to pan, placing fillets on top. Cover and cook for 20 minutes over medium heat. Carefully transfer to a glass serving dish. Top with onions. Cover and refrigerate. Serve cold. Serves 6.

Fish Patties in Tomato Sauce

2 lbs. (1 kg.) fish fillets	½ tsp. pepper
1 onion	½ tsp. paprika
4 eggs	1-2 tsp. salt
½ cup matzah meal	oil

Grind fish and onion. Add remaining ingredients. Form patties. Heat oil in skillet and fry patties, turning when light brown. When done, transfer to a large saucepan and cover with the following sauce:

¼ cup tomato paste	dash pepper
2 Tbsp. sugar	1 cup water
½ tsp. salt	1 Tbsp. *einbren* (optional, see hint)

Add water, if necessary, so that sauce will cover patties. Cook 20-30 minutes on medium flame. Refrigerate. Serve cold.

Make this einbren *and keep on hand in the refrigerator to add to sauces and soups. Heat ½ cup oil and slowly add 3 Tbsp. flour, mixing continuously with wooden spoon for 5-10 minutes until mixture becomes brown and thick. May be kept in refrigerator for weeks. Add only a tablespoon or 2 to each recipe.*

Chopped Herring Salad

1 lb. (450 gm.) pickled herring	2 Tbsp. bread crumbs
2 small onions	1 tsp. lemon juice (or vinegar)
2 tart apples	1 tsp. oil
1 hard-boiled egg	

Soak herring in cold water for at least 3 hours. Remove bones and chop fish. Chop onions, apples and egg together. Add fish and chop until mixture is smooth. Add bread crumbs, lemon juice and oil. Mix well. Serves 4-6.

Mock Chopped Herring

1 can sardines	2 Tbsp. vinegar
2 tart apples	1 tsp. salt
2 hard-boiled eggs	1-2 Tbsp. sugar
1 small raw onion	bread crumbs or matzah meal
1 slice dry bread	

The numerical equivalent of the Hebrew word for fish — דג — is seven. Therefore fish is appropriate food for the seventh day.

(Ohr HaShabbos)

Grind the first 4 ingredients together and then the dry bread. Add vinegar, salt and sugar to taste. Add bread crumbs as needed until all liquid is absorbed. Mix well. Refrigerate for at least 3 hours. Serves 4-6.

Fish Salad

2 lbs. (1 kg.) halibut, cod or similar filleted fish	DRESSING:
1 onion	¾ cup mayonnaise
1 bay leaf	1 cup chopped celery
1 slice lemon	½ cup ketchup or chili sauce
½ tsp. salt	1 Tbsp. lemon juice
2 cups water	3 hard-boiled eggs, chopped

Place first 6 ingredients in a pot. Bring to a boil, continue cooking for 15-20 minutes. Remove fish and break into small pieces; combine dressing ingredients. Mix and refrigerate. Serves 6-8.

Tuna Salad Supreme

1 can tuna, flaked	1-2 stalks celery, chopped
2 hard-boiled eggs, coarsely chopped	pinch of salt
1 small onion, chopped	2 Tbsp. mayonnaise

Mix until creamy. Serve in custard cups or in green pepper rings. Garnish with olives.

Shabbos is especially conducive to teaching Torah, since the Torah was given by G-d to Israel on Shabbos.
(The Skulener Rebbe)

Greek Salad

6 cups coarsely shredded cabbage or kohlrabi	10 slices herring & brine, cut into pieces
2 stalks celery, diced	⅓ cup vinegar
1 green pepper, diced	⅓ cup sugar
2 carrots, sliced thin	¼ lb. black olives
2 tomatoes, chopped	⅓ cup oil
1 onion, diced	salt
	pepper

Combine first 6 vegetables. Add salt and pepper and toss. Pour herring and brine over vegetables. Shake oil, sugar and vinegar in closed jar and pour over salad. Garnish with olives. Marinate and refrigerate for at least 24 hours.

When Rabbi Israel Baal Shem Tov had to choose among three places of residence, he decided upon Mezhybozh because fish are readily available there, easy to obtain in order to honor the Sabbath.
(Ohr HaShabbos)

Halibut and Avocado Salad

1½-2 lbs. (1 kg.) cooked halibut,
  in small pieces
8 hard-boiled eggs, quartered
1 large avocado, cut in
  small pieces

DRESSING:
About 1-2 cups Russian dressing
(see p. 89) made with ketchup,
mayonnaise, salt, pepper and
garlic powder, to taste

Toss everything together and serve on bed of lettuce. (Add eggs last so they do not soften). Serves 8.

It is a mitzvah to eat fish at every Sabbath meal as long as fish does not affect one adversely.

(*Kitzur Shulchan Arukh*)

Tuna Macaroni Salad

8 oz. (250 gm.) macaroni
  (preferably bows)
1 7 oz. (200 gm.) can tuna
4 Tbsp. oil
2 Tbsp. vinegar
1 small carrot, shredded
1 Tbsp. minced onion

2 Tbsp. chopped green pepper
pinch sugar
pinch pepper
salt if necessary
1 Tbsp. snipped fresh dill
  (optional)

Cook macaroni in salted water till just barely tender. Drain. Toss with remaining ingredients.
Variation: In place of the vinegar and oil, use about ½-cup of mayonnaise.

Mandarin Macaroni Salad

1 cup mayonnaise
2 Tbsp. water
2 Tbsp. lemon juice
1 Tbsp. sugar
½ tsp. salt

3 cups cooked elbow macaroni,
  drained
3 mandarin oranges or tangerines,
  sectioned

We eat fish three times on the Sabbath — once for each of our forefathers — Abraham, Isaac, and Jacob.

(*Ohr HaShabbos*)

Stir mayonnaise, water, lemon juice, sugar and salt in large bowl. Add rest of ingredients and toss to coat well. Cover. Chill at least 2 hours. Serves 10-12.

Oriental Egg Salad

1 cup cooked rice
1 large potato, cooked and mashed
4 hard-boiled eggs (2 mashed,
   2 sliced)
⅓ cup mayonnaise

1 Tbsp. chopped onion
1 Tbsp. dried chopped parsley
2 Tbsp. chopped pimento
1 Tbsp. chopped green pepper
salt and pepper, to taste

Combine all ingredients except 2 sliced eggs. Chill. Serve garnished with egg slices.

Deviled Eggs

6 hard-boiled eggs, shelled
1 Tbsp. mayonnaise
1 tsp. vinegar
dash of pepper

¾ tsp. prepared mustard
¼ tsp. salt
paprika

Carefully halve eggs and remove yolks. Force yolks through sieve or mash. Add other ingredients, except paprika. Refill egg whites, fluffing filling. Sprinkle with paprika. Cover well with plastic wrap.

Prevent eggs from cracking while boiling by adding a heaping teaspoon of salt to the water. If during boiling an egg cracks, add a little vinegar to the water to seal the egg.

Gazpacho

A refreshing cross between a soup and a salad.

1½ cups tomato juice
½ cup water
1 large ripe tomato, peeled and
   diced
3 Tbsp. chopped onion
2 Tbsp. chopped green pepper
¼ cup chopped cucumber

1 Tbsp. olive oil
2 Tbsp. vinegar
1 clove garlic
1 tsp. Worcestershire sauce
salt
pepper

Blend all ingredients until smooth. Chill well. Taste and spice as necessary. Serve with dishes of additional vegetables and croutons for garnish.

To prevent hard-boiled eggs from crumbling when sliced, wet the knife before each cut.

Rice & Fruit Pudding

3 cups cooked rice
½ cup sugar
½ tsp. salt
2 tsp. vanilla
3 Tbsp. water
4 tsp. lemon juice

8 eggs
cinnamon
1½ cups raisins
3 medium-sized apples, diced
   (or substitute other fruit)

Mix everything together and bake in well greased 9 inch by 13 inch pan at 350° F (175° C) until firm.

Fruit Soup

3 apples
3 pears
3 peaches
1 cup strawberries, hulled and
   halved or seedless grapes
juice of one lemon

2 cups orange juice
5 cups water
1 Tbsp. sugar
1 Tbsp. cornstarch
½ cup wine

Boil sugar and water. Peel and core apples and pears and dip into lemon juice to prevent discoloration. Dice apples, pears and peaches. Add to boiling water. Add whole grapes or strawberries. Simmer for 5 minutes. Add orange juice. Dissolve cornstarch with 2 Tbsp. cold water and stir into soup. Simmer, stirring gently for a few minutes and remove from heat. Allow to cool, then chill. Just before serving, add wine.

Easy Fruit Soup

peaches
plums
nectarines
apples
pears
grapes

pitted cherries or strawberries
   for color
water
1 tsp. lemon juice
½ cup sugar
1 cup orange juice

Select whatever fruits are available. Cut in small pieces to make 3-4 cups of fruit, about 3½ lb. (1½ kg.). Cover with water and simmer covered for ½ hour. While hot, add lemon juice, sugar and orange juice. Serve ice cold. Serves 5-7.

The Baal Shem Tov and some of his disciples once spent the Sabbath in a small village. The head of the community there was known for his Shalosh Seudoth. Jews from neghboring villages would come every week to partake of food and drink at this man's table and sing songs of praise to G-d. The Baal Shem Tov asked the host why he chose to invest so much in this particular mitzvah. He replied: "I have heard Jews wish that when the time comes for their soul to depart, they be among Jews. I also know that on the Sabbath we possess an additional soul, which leaves at the day's end. In order to ensure that this soul may also depart surrounded by many Jews, I gather together as many of my fellows as possible."

(Ohr HaShabbos)

Strawberry Soup

4 cups strawberries, hulled and
   checked
1 cup sugar
4 Tbsp. lemon juice

2 tsp. grated lemon peel
1 cup white wine
1 orange, without peel or pits
3 cups water

Put all ingredients in a blender jar, leaving out some or all of water if necessary. Blend till uniformly liquid. Add remaining water. Chill and serve in goblets or soup bowls.

Chilled Cantaloupe Peach Soup

6 medium-sized ripe peaches
¼ cup dry white wine
6 Tbsp. fresh lemon juice
2 Tbsp. honey

¼ tsp. cinnamon
dash nutmeg
1 medium-sized ripe cantaloupe
1 cup fresh orange juice

"Cast my lot with those who eat three meals on the Sabbath!"
(Talmud Bavli)

Peel, pit and slice peaches. Place in heavy saucepan with everything except cantaloupe and orange juice. Heat to a boil. Lower to a simmer. Cover and let stew 10 minutes. Let cool to room temperature. Blend mixture and put in a large bowl. Chop ¾ of the cantaloupe and purée with orange juice until smooth. Add to peach purée. Mince remaining melon and add. Cover and chill. Serve very cold. Serves 4.

Eggplant Slices

2 long eggplants, sliced crosswise,
   ¼-inch to ½-inch wide
salt
¼ cup tomato sauce

fresh chopped parsley, or
   dried parsley
2 cloves garlic, crushed, ½ tsp.
   garlic powder
½ tsp. salt
¼ tsp. pepper

Rabbi Shimon ben Pazi said in the name of Rabbi Yehoshua ben Levi that Bar Kapra said: "He who eats three meals on the Sabbath is spared three types of suffering: The travails that precede the Messiah, the judgment of Gehinnom, and the war of Gog and Magog."
(Talmud Bavli)

Salt eggplant slices. After a ½ hour, rinse and blot dry. Deep fry in oil. Place on absorbent towels to get rid of excess oil. Mix remaining ingredients. Smear 1 teaspoonful of sauce mixture on each slice of fried eggplant. Place slices on cookie sheet, taking care they do not touch each other. Bake in hot oven for 10 minutes. Pour off excess oil. Place slices in serving dish. Cool and serve cold with slices of challah. Serves 6-8.

MELAVEH MALKAH

It is customary to accord the departing Sabbath Queen the honor of one additional meal to be eaten after *havdalah*. Technically, one may discharge this obligation even by eating some fruit. But, how much more esteem for our beloved guest is shown by setting a proper table and partaking of one more feast before returning to the week's work!

This tradition is said to have originated with King David, who knew that he would die on the Sabbath day. Each week, at the conclusion of the Sabbath, he would celebrate the gift of life with a splendid repast.

Today, the ways in which Jews carry on this tradition run the gamut from specially prepared meat dishes, to dairy casseroles, company spreads and light snack foods.

Felafel

1 lb. (450 gm.) chickpeas	2 tsp. salt
⅓-½ loaf dry challah or bread, soaked in water	2 pieces hot pepper (optional)
	1 onion (optional)
½ head garlic	1 tsp. coriander (kuzbara)
1 Tbsp. cumin	2 tsp. baking powder

Soak chickpeas overnight. Drain and check. Grind in a meat grinder. Squeeze out water from bread and grind with garlic, onion and hot pepper. Stir in cumin, salt, coriander, and baking powder. Chill mixture for an hour or so. Form into 1-inch (2 cm.) balls. Heat oil and deep fry balls until brown. Drain, serve hot in pita with finely cut vegetable salad and tehina sauce.

Tehina Sauce

1 cup tehina (unprepared)	OPTIONAL SPICES:
1 cup water	1 tsp. salt
2 tsp. lemon juice or more, to taste	chopped parsley
	cumin
2 cloves garlic, crushed or garlic powder	paprika

Pour tehina into blender jar. Add water and rest of ingredients to taste. Blend. Can also be mixed by hand.

136

Pizza

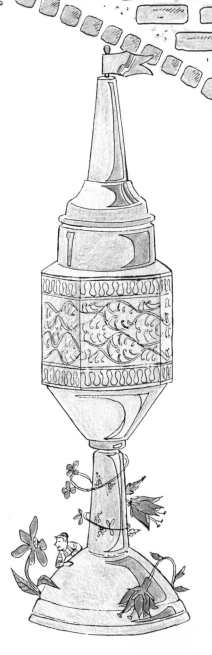

DOUGH:
2 cups flour
1 tsp. baking powder
½ tsp. salt
⅓ cup oil
⅓ cup juice or milk
1 egg

SAUCE:
½ cup tomato paste

½ cup water
1 tsp. salt
dash of pepper
2 Tbsp. oil
1 tsp. oregano

TOPPING:
2 cups shredded yellow
    processed cheese

Combine ingredients for dough and knead until soft. Divide dough in half. Roll dough thinly (⅛ inch) and place in 2 baking pans. Mix sauce ingredients and spread half on each pizza. Sprinkle 1 cup cheese on each pizza. Bake at 350° F (175° C) for 20 minutes. Makes 16 wedges.
Variations: Chopped olives, sliced onions, peppers, tomatoes and/or mushrooms can be added on top of cheese.

Cheese Savory

7-8 slices bread
8 slices processed cheese
3 eggs
2 cups milk

¼ cup sherry (optional)
½ tsp. each: salt, paprika,
    mustard powder

Layer bread and cheese in a greased casserole. Mix the remaining ingredients and pour over bread and cheese. Bake at 325° F (150° C) for 1 hour. Serves 6.

Curried Spaghetti

8 oz. (250 gm.) spaghetti, cooked and drained	½ tsp. thyme
1 3 oz. (100 gm.) can button mushrooms, with liquid	2 cans condensed celery soup, or substitute*
1 tsp. curry powder	¼ cup milk
1½ tsp. grated onions	bread crumbs, grated cheese —
¼ tsp. oregano	for topping

Combine first eight ingredients in 2½ quart casserole. Sprinkle with bread crumbs and cheese. Bake uncovered at 350° F (175° C) till hot and bubbly, about a ½ hour. (To make this a full meal, add 2 7-oz. (200 gm.) cans of tuna, flaked, before baking).

* To substitute dry celery soup mix, combine 2 packets with 2 cups water in a saucepan. Stir while bringing to a boil. When mixture boils, add 1 cup milk. Remove from heat.

Lasagna

1 Tbsp. oil	¾ tsp. oregano
4 Tbsp. minced onion	1 lb. (450 gm.) lasagna noodles
24 oz. (800 gm.) tomato purée	1 lb. (450 gm.) yellow cheese, grated or sliced
6 oz. (180 gm.) mushroom slices	
1 cup water	1 lb. (450 gm.) or more cottage
1½ tsp. salt	or similar cheese

Sauté onion in oil until transparent. Add tomato sauce, mushrooms, water and seasonings. Simmer for 15 minutes, stirring occasionally. Heat oven to 375° F (180° C). Cook noodles till just tender; drain. Spoon a thin layer of sauce into a greased 9 inch by 13 inch pan. Cover with a layer of lasagna noodles. Spoon ¼ of cottage cheese over this, ¼ of yellow cheese. Repeat three more times. Cover and bake 40-45 minutes. Grate more cheese on top, if desired. Uncover and bake 5 more minutes. Serves 8.

As the Sabbath leaves us, we sing "Hamavdil" and ask that both offspring and the means to support them be granted us aplenty — like the sand at the seashore, like the stars at night.

Rabbi Simeon ben Lakish said: "On the eve of the Sabbath, the Holy One, blessed be He, gives man an additional soul, and at the termination of the Sabbath, he withdraws it from him."

(Talmud Bavli)

A pot with hard-to-remove cooked-on food is easier to clean if you boil a little water in it with 1 Tbsp. salt or scouring powder.

Tomato Quiche

1 9-inch baked pie crust
1½ cups grated cheese
1 medium onion, sliced
1 Tbsp. butter
salt and pepper to taste
¼ lb. (100 gm.) tomatoes, sliced

4 eggs
1½ cups milk
3 Tbsp. flour
¼ tsp. salt
paprika

Sauté onions in butter with salt and pepper. Cover crust with cheese. Cover cheese with onions and tomatoes. Beat eggs, milk, flour and salt together well to form custard. Pour custard over onions and tomatoes. Sprinkle with paprika. Bake at 375° F (190° C) for 40-45 minutes or until firm when jiggled.
For extra convenience: make pie dough, shape in pan and freeze before Shabbos. Defrost it while preparing filling and custard.

Cheese Bourekas

DOUGH:
3½ cups flour
½ lb. (200 gm.) salted margarine
6 oz. buttermilk or sour cream
 or 1 container eshel
sesame seeds

FILLING:
½ lb. (225 gm.) salty white
 (feta) cheese
2 eggs

One should sing and rejoice in the Sabbath as it says, "The statutes of the Al-mighty are just, gladdening the heart." Therefore it has become customary to sing songs and praises at the Sabbath meals. Certainly this honors the Sabbath and honors the Sabbath meals as it is befitting to rejoice with royalty as it arrives and departs.

(Commentary on Yeish Nochalim)

Mix flour and margarine well, then add buttermilk or eshel. Form dough into a ball. In a separate bowl, combine cheese and eggs. Sprinkle counter surface with sesame seeds. Roll dough thinly on sesame seeds. Cut circles with a glass. Put a heaping teaspoon of filling on each circle. Fold in half, pinching closed. Bake on a greased baking sheet at 350° F (175° C) until light brown.

To prepare more quickly, divide dough into fourths. Roll into rectangles and spread a quarter of the filling in the center of each. Fold sides over cheese filling. Roll. Slice rolls after baking.

To clean hard water sediment from pots, boil a little vinegar in them. The sediment should then wash right off. For stubborn cases, repeat.

Pineapple Square

1 lg. can crushed pineapple, drained   juice of 1 lemon
5 Tbsp. flour   3 eggs
½ tsp. salt   1½ Tbsp. margarine

Mix crushed pineapple, flour, salt and lemon juice. Beat eggs until light in color and add to flour mixture. Melt margarine in a square pan. Bake at 350° F (180° C) for 45 minutes. Serve hot.

The prayer "*Veyiten Lecha,*" which is recited when the Sabbath ends, is conducive to bringing upon those who recite it the blessing of a good livelihood.

(*Ohr HaShabbos*)

Cheese Kugel

4 oz. (100 gm.) margarine   1 handful raisins
3 eggs   8 oz. (200 gm.) cooked noodles
2 cups milk   1 can crushed pineapple,
½ cup sugar   well drained
8 oz. (200 gm.) cottage cheese   crushed cornflakes, or a mixture
1 tsp. vanilla   of sugar and cinnamon

Melt margarine in a 9 inch by 13 inch pan in oven and cool. Beat the eggs and combine with rest of ingredients. Pour into pan. Sprinkle cornflakes on top. Bake 1 hour at 350° F (175° C).

Rabbi Elimelech of Lizensk advised women especially to partake of Melaveh Malkah, saying out loud that they are eating in order to fulfill the mitzvah of Melaveh Malkah. This is deemed conducive to easy childbirth.

(*Ohr HaShabbos*)

Cheese Blintze Supreme

12 frozen cheese or fruit blintzes   1 tsp. vanilla
2 pints sour cream (2 *shamenet*   ¼ cup orange juice
   containers)   4 eggs
½ cup sugar

Grease 3 quart pyrex dish and place blintzes (1 layer) about 1-inch apart. Mix remaining ingredients in a bowl and pour over blintzes. Bake at 350° F (175°C) for 1 hour uncovered. A rich main course or can be served as a dessert.

Cheese Cake

BAKED CRUST:

1½ **cups flour**
½ **cup margarine**
½ **cup sugar**
1 **egg yolk**
½ **cup juice**

Combine all ingredients. Roll out dough on a round springform or 9 inch by 13 inch rectangular pan. Bake for 20 minutes at 350° F (175° C).

NO BAKE COOKIE CRUMB CRUST:

Blend 12 oz. (300 gm.) cookie crumbs with 5 Tbsp. melted margarine. Pat down on bottom of pan. *Don't bake.* Place in freezer while you prepare cheese mixture.

FILLING:

1 lb. (500 gm.) **white spreading cheese**
½ **cup sour cream**
5 **eggs, separated**
1 **cup sugar**
rind of 1 lemon
1 **tsp. vanilla**
⅓ **cup flour**
⅓ **cup cornstarch**

Combine cheese, sour cream, egg yolks, ½ cup sugar, lemon rind, vanilla, flour and cornstarch. Beat until smooth. Beat egg whites with remaining ½ cup sugar and fold into cheese mixture. Pour filling onto the crust. Bake at 300° F (150° C) for 1¼ hours.

Make an unusual spice holder by sticking whole cloves into an esrog (citron). The skin of the esrog is very thick, so pierce it with a thick needle, an awl or a thin screwdriver before you insert each clove.

A medium-sized esrog needs approximately 4 oz. (120 gm.) of cloves, stuck in as closely together as possible. Once you start this project, you should finish it within 2-3 days or the esrog will spoil before you're done.

Blintze Cake

BATTER:	FILLING:
1 cup butter	2 lbs. (1 kg.) cottage or
½ cup sugar	farmer cheese
4 eggs	½ cup sugar
1½ cups flour	2 eggs
4 tsp. baking powder	1 tsp. vanilla or lemon extract
¾ tsp. salt	

Melt butter in a 9 inch by 13 inch pan. Pour into a bowl and add remaining batter ingredients, mixing quickly. In a second bowl, combine filling ingredients. Spoon half the batter into the pan. Pour over it all the filling. Spoon remaining batter over filling. Bake at 300° F (150° C) for 1¼-1½ hours.

Bananas Foster

An elegant dessert, combining hot butter syrup, ice cream and fresh bananas

4 large or 6 medium yellow bananas	½ cup butter
lemon juice	cinnamon
1 cup brown sugar	6 scoops ice cream

Peel bananas and halve lengthwise. Brush with lemon juice. Combine brown sugar and butter in a saucepan. Heat gently until melted. Add bananas. Cook 1 minute. Sprinkle with cinnamon. Put scoops of your favorite flavor ice cream in each of 6 dessert cups. Pour banana syrup over the ice cream and serve immediately. Serves 6.

142

Popovers

1 cup milk
3 eggs
½ tsp. salt

2 tsp. butter
1 cup flour

Combine all ingredients in a blender jar. Blend on low speed, then for a few seconds on high. Fill well-greased 12-muffin tin. Bake for 10 minutes in hot 450° F (225° C) oven, then 40 minutes more at 350° F (175° C). Turn out and serve immediately with butter or any spread.

Whole Wheat Muffins

2 cups whole wheat flour
1 tsp. baking soda
¼ cup sugar
1 tsp. cinnamon
½ tsp. salt

½ cup raisins (optional)
1 egg, beaten
1 cup buttermilk, yogurt or
  sour milk
2 Tbsp. oil

Mix all dry ingredients thoroughly, including raisins. Make a well in center and add egg, milk and oil. Stir ONLY until dry ingredients are moist. Fill greased muffin tins half full. Bake at 375° F (185° C) for about 15 minutes. Makes about 12-15 muffins. *Variation:* Omit 1 cup flour and replace with oats, bran or wheat germ.

Rabbi Chanina said: "Set your table at the termination of the Sabbath even if you eat no more than just a bite."

(Talmud Bavli)

Polish Greetz (a Meat Dish)

½ cup beans
½ cup barley
2 cups sliced vegetables (carrots,
  potatoes, squash, onions)
2-3 quarts (2-3 liters) water
8 chicken pieces
salt

pepper
fresh garlic
paprika
soup greens
3 Tbsp. oatmeal or soup powder
  to thicken
soup bones

Clean and check beans and barley. Soak over Shabbos. Afterwards cook all ingredients together for at least 2 hours. Serve steaming hot. Serves 8. A meal in a bowl, guaranteed to warm you up on even the coldest winter evening.

Throughout the Jewish world, we sing of Eliyahu HaNavi at the close of the Sabbath, since he is the harbinger who will precede Mashiach. We have been promised that Eliyahu will not come on the eve of a Sabbath or holiday because people are so preoccupied... rather, this bearer of good tidings will come to us after a Sabbath, since in the merit of the Sabbath, the L-rd will send our Redeemer.

(Sefer HaManhig)

143

INSIDE AISH HATORAH

At Aish HaTorah in Jerusalem, every student has an opportunity to become aware of the depth and beauty of his Jewish heritage. It is a special place where people discover that Judaism is meaningful and very relevant to their own lives. From the "Explorations" — Introductory Program through Rabbinic Ordination, the goal is the same — to instill a commitment to Jewish survival and a feeling of responsibility to the Jewish People.

Founded in 1974 by Rabbi Noah Weinberg, Aish HaTorah-EYAHT is providing Jewish men and women with an opportunity to discover a new sense of pride in their heritage through a meaningful understanding of Torah and traditional values of Jewish living.

Aish HaTorah College of Jewish Studies
1 Shvut St.
POB 14149
Jewish Quarter, Old City
Jerusalem, Israel
Telephone: (02) 273-191
Dean: Rabbi Noah Weinberg

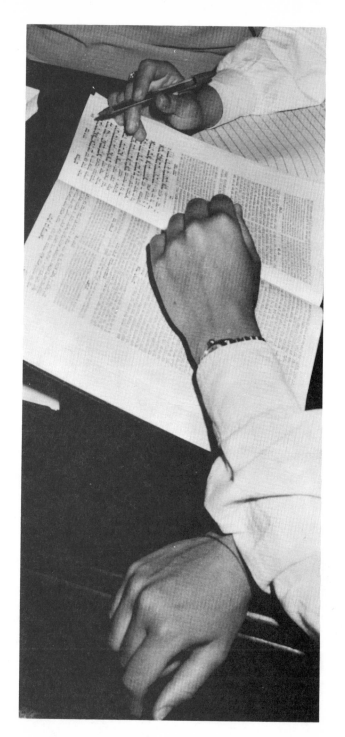

148

EYAHT — Aish HaTorah College of Jewish Studies for Women — is dedicated to helping each woman reach her maximum potential and become a vital link in the chain which binds the great Jewish women of our past to those of our future.

EYAHT (acronym for the Hebrew: A woman who knows G-d shall be praised. Proverbs 31) offers an exciting, stimulating environment with full-time and part-time courses for all levels from beginner to advanced. The friendly, congenial atmosphere is an excellent place for the inquisitive student to discover the relevance of her Jewish heritage.

EYAHT
Aish HaTorah College for Women
22 Imrei Binah St.
Kiryat Sanz
Jerusalem, Israel
Telephone: (02) 823522
Dean: Rebetzin Denah Weinberg

149

Aish HaTorah-Jerusalem also serves as home base for an extensive outreach network that sponsors educational programs, seminars and Jewish events throughout North and South America, Europe and Israel.

MAIN OFFICE
1 Shvut Street
POB 14149, Jewish Quarter
Old City, Jerusalem
(02) 273-155

BRANCHES
St. Louis
7731 Wild Plum
St. Louis, MO 63130
(314) 862-2474
New York
151 W. 25th Street
New York, NY 10001
(212) 929-0500

Great Britain
23 Hereford Road
Liverpool L15 9HJ
44 (51) 734-0212

Los Angeles
10100 Santa Monica Blvd. Suite 550
Los Angeles, CA 90067
(213) 556-3054

New Jersey
900 Forest Avenue
Lakewood, NJ 08701
(201) 370-9053

Toronto
296A Wilson Avenue
Downsview, Ontario M3H 158
(416) 636-7530

Brazil
Maestro Francisco Braga 420/201
Copacabana, Rio de Janeiro 22041

Index